GENOCIDE AGAINST THE TUTSI

TERRORIZED IN
RWANDA

Healed By Grace

ANAMALIYA

Book Cover Credit: Michael Scott

Back Cover Photo Credit: Gabriella Mukakabano @Kabanocompany

Printed in the United States of America

Dedication

I *dedicate my book to my brother Sylvestre Nkubili. Nkubili, you were a kind and brilliant human being, and an exceptional journalist. Your dream didn't perish with you, it is alive within all of us. I lit the torch of your hope and dreams and your daughters Carine and Aurore will follow. Your oldest daughter Carine is an amazing writer - how I wish you could see your beautiful and smart girls!*

To my parents, Athanase and Verediane: what you sowed in your children lives on. I can assure you the values and love you instilled in me will be carried on to my sons.

To my sons, Alexander and Azariah. I am so thankful that God chose me to be your mom. I am grateful that He used you to save me from the road of self-destruction. You are the reason I don't give up. You are the reason I get up every morning. God has bestowed so many blessings on you, I can't wait to see them coming to life.

To my sister, Christina, on behalf of my nieces and my parents, I want to thank you for all that you did for all of us! If God had not spared your life, I don't know what would have happened to Carine, Aurore, and myself or your daughter Gabriella. Your sacrifice, hard work, and selfless love are an example of how a God-fearing woman lives out her life. It will be a legacy to my children. You didn't only teach us, you lived by example. I cannot count how many times your words were a voice of reason in my thoughts and decision-making. Watching you helped me turn my life around and gave me the strength to go on, when all the power in me wanted to give up. You may be 5'2 but you are a giant in our eyes! Thank you from the bottom of my heart.

To the community of genocide survivors, this life is a gift we have from above. Don't let it pass by while living in bitterness or by being unforgiving and fearful. I believe with all my heart that we have been given a second chance to glorify God. Let go of all the strongholds and let Jesus shine your life to all mankind.

Acknowledgments

First and foremost, I would like to thank my Jesus, my Savior, my Father the Highest God. Because of my God, I have been given a second chance at life. With my love of my savior, I am able to present you, "Terrorized in Rwanda, Healed by Grace", thereby allowing you to learn about my story. May your name be glorified throughout all the earth. May all who read my story find love, comfort, redemption, and healing, just as I did.

My intelligent and gorgeous niece Carine Umuhumuza and my precious sister Christina Mukankaka - without your hard work and tireless nights helping with the editing of my book, there will be no book to read! You challenge me and inspire me to be the woman I am today! You are my beating heart and I am glad God made us a family! I adore both of you dearly! Cheers to many books in the near future! And *here to you Maman* who could not read but gave birth to strong and smart women!

Michelle Hill - You are the best mentor a girl could have. It is you who made it happen, otherwise, I would not have found VicToria. Thank you for all the time you took to guide me through this journey. Your knowledge about book publishing is astounding. May Almighty add another precious stone on your mansion in Heaven!

Anyango Reggy my first editor - Your kind words and encouragement after you read my story that's what encouraged me to keep writing. You took a chance on me and patiently read and edited without judgment. Instead, you showed me love and encouragement. Your soothing words gave me courage to continue. Thank you with all my heart.

Darla Burtos and to Chantal Kayitesi who connected us - Thank you both so much for encouraging me to tell my story. Darla, thank you immensely for the sacrifice you took editing my book.

Lonzen and Fidelis - Thank you both so much for protecting, supporting, and loving me without condemning me when I needed you most. Lonzen, thank you for the history lesson and for making me laugh with your silly jokes.

Jane and Dick Kaufman - You are my family! Thank you so much for your love, generosity, and for welcoming five strangers who didn't even speak your language into your home and treating them like your own. Jane, my first English teacher, you are still the best teacher by far. Words cannot express how much I feel about you both.

Sue and Frank Robb, Craig and Cyndie Gardner and Marcella and Ernst Lutz - Thank you for loving me without judgment and modeling Christ so well! I cannot ever thank you enough! All of you are a gift from above! May God reward each of you for your kindness and the love you possess for His people.

To each and every one of you who held my hands when God was molding me - I cannot list all the names but you all know who you are. I will forever be grateful to all of you.

Table of Contents

PART I: Memories

PART II: Terror

PART III: Aftermath

PART IV: Exodus

PART V: Healing

Author's Note

Dear sons and daughters of the Most High God,

    I am grateful and humbled that you are interested enough to pick up my book. This book contains my story unedited, unfiltered. My pain, my mistakes, my failures, my victories and the Grace of God. It is about my own experience in the genocide and afterwards, my struggles to make sense of senseless acts. It is about my romantic relationships, or the lack of them, depending on how you look at it.

    I am able to share both my darkest experiences and some of the embarrassing events in my life because I finally found healing and am no longer a prisoner of my past. What used to be a stronghold is now good news and I wanted to share what God has done for me. I pray my story, my vulnerability and my exposed heart will help you see that there's a God who is bigger than any pain, failure, and disappointment you will go through in this life. I pray God will use my story to bring healing to those who read my book

    In the beginnings of the book, I briefly touch on the history of Rwanda as I've learned or read it, just enough to place my own story. Please note, this is no way my expertise or my focus. There are many resources available for those who want to learn more. This book is about my personal journey.

Thank you so much and may God bless you.

Anamaliya

PART I: Memories
Chapter 1

"Do not be anxious about anything, but in every situation, by prayer and petition, with thanksgiving, present your requests to God. And the peace of God, which transcends all understanding, will guard your hearts and your minds in Christ Jesus."

~ Philippians 4:6-7

It is amazing how, when your life turns upside-down, a lifetime of events flashes through your mind. The good, the bad, and the ugly memories you would rather bury in your conscience, never to be remembered, reel through your mind with no stop or pause button.

In mid-2006, while I was living in the small town of Dover, New Hampshire, pregnant and alone in my mid-twenties, my mind took me back to 1994 during the genocide, when I was running for my life.

Layers of pain consumed me. Memories from a past I had tried to forget seeped into the present until I throbbed with hurt. I wished I could escape or that I had a cave I could crawl into never to be seen or heard from again. The memories of the past consumed my days. Sometimes I was glad for those memories because they helped me to ignore the loneliness, heartbreak, and misery I felt in the present. There were times I wondered if I would ever experience heartfelt laughter again.

I remembered my beloved country Rwanda with its beautiful blue sky and green hills. The banana plantations and melodic sound of birds singing in the avocado and banana trees. Oh, how I adored the summertime, the smell of berries in the bushes all around me and ripe bananas. Wheat growing in the open plains, sweet potatoes in the valleys, and corn and beans dressed the fields of my home. Coffee and tea plantations clothed the hills of my love, Rwanda. There, the night was a vision on its own. We had cattle grazing on hills and herders singing for them. The voices of children playing games was so soothing! My village was perfect. Though its people were poor, they didn't know any other life, so we shared what we had. You don't often desire what is unknown to you.

When my parents had a bountiful harvest they used to spread our crops among our relatives and friends. The neighbor's kids didn't go to bed hungry. Sharing was simply the way of life. I remembered my beautiful mother with her musical laughter and my father who looked at her as if she were a precious jewel. I longed to have my mother around and to feel her warm hugs. She had a way of making each child feel as though they were her only child, even though we were eight children: five boys and three girls.

At times, I thought about my innocence as a child and I wondered how my father would have felt about me being pregnant with no husband in the picture. I could imagine the disappointment in his face. I remembered my father's integrity and how he taught us good values; how he disliked rebellious actions. On those days, I was glad that they would never see me as I was. I loved my parents and I wanted them to be proud of me. I didn't want them to see that all the values I had been taught as a child had been ignored and overruled by desires that would eventually lead me to make some wrong choices. Choices that would affect me and the child I was carrying for the rest of our lives.

As a child, I used to think that if either of my parents died for any reason, I would not be able to survive. My parents had been the center of my life. The mutual respect and love they had for one another was something I greatly admired. Even as a child, when other kids would ask me which parent was my favorite, my answer was that I wouldn't be able to pick only one – they were both my favorite. Each of my parents was unique and held a special role in my life. I loved them both equally.

My mother had devoted her whole life to us, her children. Every morning she would get up and warm my water because I broke into hives when I used cold water to bathe. We didn't even have electricity then. She had to light up the stove with coals, a strenuous task to do morning after morning. And every time we came home from school, we found a hot meal waiting for us.

She was always eager to listen to us when we needed her. There was not a waking moment that I longed for my mother to be there, because she was always there. I still think my mother was the most beautiful woman inside and out: small in height, beautiful brown skin, gentle with a heart of gold, a love for people, a melodious laugh, and warm hugs. If I could personify "happiness", it was my mother with her child-like spirit. I had never met anyone who disliked my mother. She was the true heart of our home.

Slender and over 6 feet, my father was as handsome as my mother was beautiful. My father was an incredible man, full of integrity and respected by everyone. When my father was around, our home was filled with a sense of peace and protection. I knew nothing could harm me when he was there. He was very strict, but at the same time, very loving and playful. My father was the breadwinner of the family; always eager to work hard enough to provide for us all.

I never saw him sleep past five in the morning. I don't think he knew anything about being idle. He was always on the move. Men came seeking counsel from him and women having a hard time in their homes came to seek protection. He was both tough and gentle; my inspiration in life. My father loved God as best as he knew how. He neither started a day without going to morning Mass nor went to bed without praying.

When I was young, I loved going to Catholic Mass with father. Also, I loved the treats afterward, candies and soda. But I especially loved the stories he told me when we were alone. I always looked forward to going with him to church.

However, as I grew up and merged into adolescence, sleep was more important than the treats and stories. He would get up, get ready, and then tell me to get up so I could go to Mass with him. I would insist that I didn't feel well and promise to go the next time, but next time turned out to be never which I came to regret. Now that he is dead, I wish I could have spent more time with my father, whom I loved dearly.

My mother and father were true soulmates. I never saw them angry at each other. They were partners in everything, including discipline: they never disagreed in how to discipline us. We were lucky if our mother didn't tell our father when we had disobeyed her during the day while he was not around. Otherwise, it would have meant double the trouble. My father never asked my mother how or why we needed to be reprimanded. He always said if someone disciplined us, it was because we deserved it. My father never undermined her decisions. He truly loved and respected my mother.

In my neighborhood, there was a family whose father had abandoned them at a young age. As far as I could remember, I had always seen them alone with only a mother to provide for them. There were three boys and one girl. Their mother worked hard for them, but you could see that she had never healed from the pain her husband had caused her. She always had sorrow in her face and in her voice. Her children were the same way, always filled with sadness. They rarely laughed. Looking at them, I always wished that I could take their pain away.

I remember my parents telling us that we needed to be extra nice to those kids because they were so fragile. Because of this, I always appreciated my parents, loved, and admired them greatly, realizing I was fortunate to have them.

My father and mother wanted me and my siblings to succeed in life. My father emphasized the importance of education and encouraged us to seek a better life. He always said, "What are you going to become if you don't go to school?" He worked so hard to give us everything to succeed. My older siblings obeyed what my father told them, and in turn, they set examples for us. He wanted the younger children to look up to the older ones and follow in their steps.

As I reached my preteen years, I had an older brother and one older sister that I looked up to. They had completed school and were making our parents proud. My older siblings were the ones who now paid the tuition for the younger children because they felt my parents had done enough.

The strategy was, if one finished school and got a job, they had to help the others as well. With eight children, I don't think my parents could have raised us alone if the older children hadn't helped. This is a common practice in Rwanda, especially in families with a lot of children.

Taking your family in is another common practice in Rwanda. When children lose parents, the grandparents often take custody of the orphaned children. And so it was for my mother after her own mother died bringing her into this world and her father dying soon afterwards.

Her grandparents were from a different time and they didn't see the value in educating their granddaughter or sending her to school. They believed a girl was supposed to stay home to do housework until she was old enough to get married. When a law was passed in Rwanda declaring that every child must go to school, they paid money and gave gifts to bribe the local authorities so my mother would not have to go to school. At just eighteen years old, my mother was married off.

As a child I couldn't fully understand the impact illiteracy had on my mother. Growing up with five boys, all I wanted was to play soccer and run around with them. I loved being surrounded by our big family; so, my mom's illiteracy was the least of my concerns. Though I saw glimpses of it during childhood and felt sad for my mother, I never thought of it as a serious issue. It wasn't until later as an adult, having learned the pleasures of reading and writing, that I was able to understand my mother's deep desire for her daughters to get a good education; her reason for continually motivating us girls to learn to read and write.

Without the opportunity to go to school, she never learned how to read or write cursive, but she taught herself to read print and could read the newspaper. I remember writing letters for her to my sister and oldest brother. Every time she received letters from one of her older children, especially from my sister, Mother and I would go to our secret place and I would read the letter aloud to her. These were special moments for us. I always looked forward with excitement to this activity, our secret event. Now, I realize how hard those moments must have been for my mother.

I came into my parents' life when they were in their forties and after they had been raising children for over twenty years. I was like another boy compared to my older sister Christina who was very responsible.

My siblings from oldest to the youngest were: Nkubili, Sesonga, Christina, Mathias, Jean Damascene, myself, Augustin, and the last, Sylvie. Nkubili, and Christina looked more like my mother; Sesonga, Augustin, Sylvie, and Damascene were mixtures of our both parents; while Mathias and I looked more like my father.

Having been born in the middle of my brothers, I acted like one of the them. I remember how I always fought with my brother Damascene. One minute we were best friends walking around holding hands and the next minute, I would be crying. I used to follow him everywhere. When we went to play soccer, I hated how every time we played, he and his friend made me the goalkeeper. I would whine about it, but in the end, I always did what it took to play, because I wanted to hang out with him.

However, the times he wanted to hang out with his boys and didn't want his little sister around, Damascene would make me cry so that I would go home. I can still remember my mother saying, "What kind of girl are you anyway, running behind boys? Why don't you stay home like normal girls?"

Even when my mother told me to do the dishes or sweep the house, I always complained by asking why the boys couldn't do the chore, since they were older than me. My mother couldn't believe it. My brother Mathias was the peacemaker between me and Damascene, and sometimes, if Damascene made me cry, Mathias would do the same thing to him. So, when we were young, especially when we were left alone at home, it was a never-ending war between me and Damascene. We had a love-hate relationship and could always find a way to get on each other's nerves.

Sylvie was the baby of the family. I don't remember interacting with her much: most of the time she was trailing behind our mom. Augustin, my youngest brother, was very quiet and sweet-natured, and he spent most of his time playing with Sylvie. To me, she seemed like a little baby and too girly, which was boring.

Nkubili and Christina were not living at home when I was growing up. I don't know much about them as kids. I respected them as I respected my parents when they came home. I was more afraid of my oldest brother Nkubili than I was of my father. Even though he resembled my mother, my brother's character was like my father's.

Since we came later in their lives and our parents were now older, they were not as tough on us as they were with our older siblings. When my older siblings came home and saw how we were acting, they couldn't believe our parents had become that soft. The first-born,

Nkubili, used to tell us how my father was very tough on him. If my father was not home when he came back from school, no matter how late my father got home, he would wake my brother up and ask him what he learned at school. If he didn't have an answer, there would a big price to pay.

For this reason, our older siblings couldn't imagine what had happened to our parents. I guess that's what happens to the eldest children when the parents are still young and have very high expectations for their children. By the time we came into the picture, they had battled with so many children, they were tired of fighting.

Sesonga, the second-born, escaped punishment from our parents by running to our paternal grandparents. My mother used to tell me how every time my parents wanted to punish him for something he did, he would go to our grandparents. My grandfather, especially, loved my brother and always spoiled him with no retribution for his actions. In the end, Sesonga dropped out of school when he was in second grade and hid at our grandparents'.

My grandfather told my father to leave Sesonga alone, and Sesonga moved there and lived with them until they died. By the time they passed, it was too late for him to go back to school and my parents had given up on him. Sesonga was what they call the "black sheep" of the family. Sesonga was handsome, with soft, curly afro hair, and very reserved like my father. Since he spent most of my childhood outside our home I don't remember much about him. However, I do remember he loved nice clothes and would not wear anything without ironing it first. I can still see him standing and looking at himself in the mirror for hours before he left the house. Our grandfather totally spoiled him.

Our parents worked hard to instill good principles in us: to work hard, to love God, and to love and respect people and ourselves. My father didn't just *tell* us to succeed in life; he supported us in whatever we attempted to do to become successful. He never missed a school conference or a day to come see how we did at the end of a semester when we received our report cards.

Back then, in Rwanda, especially in the small towns, at the end of every semester before the holidays or school break, all the teachers and students gathered around in an open field where everyone could come to watch students receive their grades. They started with the younger grades and proceeded to the older grades. Each class waited its turn.

The teacher and the entire class stood up in the middle of the crowd, while the teacher announced the student's name, the rank in the class, and the grade received. The humiliating thing was not the letter grade you got, but the fact that your grade was announced to the entire community. On days like these, my father was always there to support us. My brothers and sister and I were celebrated when we did well and scolded when we didn't do as well as he would have liked.

I can never forget when I was in a fourth grade—I had this teacher named Madame Josephine who didn't care much about us or our education. Madame Josephine came in when she felt like it, or if there was an important visitor, like if there was going to be a superintendent in the area. This teacher was hardly ever in the classroom. She was more interested in the male teachers than in teaching us.

Once she even got caught in the classroom with another male teacher. Madame Josephine always left us with work and never stayed to see if we knew what we were doing. Consequently, careless kids, like me, took advantage of this free time and snuck out to play in the playground which was behind our class.

At the end of that first term, I learned an unforgettable lesson. When it was time to receive our grade; our teacher and the whole class got up and stood in the middle of the whole crowd there. It didn't cross my mind that what I had been doing would have consequences, I think I even got up excitedly and was walking ahead of my class. But then, my teacher began calling names: number one is so and so, number two is... and so it went all the way up to number twenty. When Madame

Josephine had passed number ten, I knew I was dead meat. I wanted to crawl in a hole and disappear. .

She continued and passed twenty-one, twenty-two; then she called my name on the twenty-third student. That term I was 23rd in the class of probably 55 kids, with 50 points. I was two points away from failing the whole term. I looked to where my father was sitting, and I saw disappointment written all over his face.

Our family was known for having smart kids. Much of my life, I had never passed number eight, even if I had done badly. No one in my family had ever passed the tenth spot, never mind reaching the twenties. At that moment, I wished my father was like other parents who didn't care about their child's grade and never came to see them. What was I going to tell my father? How was I going to face him? I felt like a disappointment to the whole family.

After all the grades were called out and the students were free to go home, I couldn't bear to look at my father. When I got near him, with my eyes facing the ground, he just looked at me and shook his head. Father was dumbfounded to the point he couldn't say anything to me, not even to yell at me. I guess he couldn't believe the outcome either. He just looked at me for a good five-minutes and chuckled. And then he said, "Let's go home and tell your mother how you did." But I didn't want to go home: I felt it was better to run away instead of telling her.

Prior to my horrendous grade, when we passed number five, my dad usually yelled at us and asked us why we couldn't have done better. He would also ask where we were when other kids were studying and paying attention. Before my embarrassing incident, I always looked forward to going home to my mom and telling her how well I did. That day, however, I went home dragging my feet because I didn't have strength to face her. In my heart, I knew I had failed her big time.

That day, Mathias and Damascene were laughing and were the ones who couldn't wait to get home and tell my mom how I had done.

To them, it was not sad—it was hysterical. They couldn't believe how I could reach up to the twenty-third spot. I lived with that humiliation for years. They had fun teasing me for a long time. I don't think that any of my family remembers my humiliation from that, but I can never forget the jokes and laughter my grades brought to my family. The incident of my school grade shocked and shook me so that by the end of the second term, I was number two in my class. After the shame of that grade, I was never again careless about my grades, regardless of the teacher.

———————

The older I got, the more I started to change. Instead of wanting to be around my father and acting like my brothers all the time, I wanted to be closer to my mother. I wanted to be like my older sister, Christina, and I wanted to make my mother happy and proud of me. I knew that if I succeeded, it would also be my mother's success. I started enjoying helping my mother and I could see her delight with my change in attitude.

She began going out more to visit her friends, because now she could count on me. She taught me how to cook simple things; if it was something complicated, she did it herself, because she knew that I was still learning. I already knew how to do basic chores—cleaning the house and doing dishes—and how I was happy to do them. My mother felt confident that I would handle my basic responsibilities.

Our house had a long fence around it that my father built it with his own hands. It was so tall that you couldn't see the house from the outside. Inside of the fence, around the side of the house, I planted flowers. I loved when these flowers started to bloom and the whole house filled with their wonderful aroma.

Outside of the fence, we had a big farm surrounding us. In the middle of that land there were hundreds of large avocado trees and a banana plantation. At the entrance of the fence, toward the left, there was a long driveway. On the right-hand side of the driveway, I planted flowers from top to bottom. There was nothing I loved more than sitting in that driveway, looking down and seeing it all swept and surrounded by colorful flowers. I felt peace and love all around me, especially in the evening when I would watch the sun set.

Our house sat on top of a hill and the view of the sunset and the sunrise was out of this world. To this day, I can clearly recall the image of the enormous, golden-orange sun as it was ascending and descending. Life was wonderful then— as a child sitting in our driveway and enjoying those warm, sunny days.

Even though it had been over twenty years and most of my family had been eliminated, during my pregnancy their memory was so strong to me, it was almost like I was reliving my childhood. However, all the wonderful memories about my siblings, my parents, and our home never lasted too long. Each time I would be awakened either by the painful reality of being pregnant and alone, or the pain of knowing that I would never see my family again.

Most of my family was wiped away by the genocide. The genocide brought a great cry to the whole country and left many of us orphans…defenseless and alone. Many of our children will never know their grandparents, aunties, uncles, or cousins.

Chapter 2

"... We rejoice in hope of the glory of God.
Not only that, but we rejoice in our sufferings,
knowing that suffering produces endurance, and
endurance produces character, and character
produces hope, and hope does not put us to
shame, because God's love has been poured into
our hearts through the Holy Spirit who has been
given to us."

~ Romans 5: 2-5

It is impossible to talk about the genocide without first talking about Rwanda's history because that history was the cause of all the conflict that has impacted the life of every Rwandese. We still live with the aftermath of that nightmare.

Rwandan history is very controversial and it is hard to truly know the truth of our origins since there are no written documents backing up the oral history. The origins of Hutu and Tutsi really are unknown and what is known often comes from stories passed on from generation to generation and, in my opinion, are biased depending on who is telling the story. Unfortunately, our history, much like the histories of many African countries, is tainted with blood and colonization.

It is told that Abatwa people, also known as Twa "pygmy" people, were natives of Rwanda and Abahutu "Hutus" and Abatutsi "Tutsis" came there when the Twa people were already living there. Not much else is known about the Twa people.

Twa people totaled up to one percent of the Rwandan population. They lived in isolated communities, most of the time in remote villages. They survived on their artistic work which was primarily pottery and dancing abilities.

Next, they say, the Hutu people followed. It is told that the Hutu are part of Bantu speaking folks from differents parts of Africa. The Hutu were farmers, estimated to be eighty-five percent of Rwandan citizens.

Finally, it is told, the Tutsis arrived in Rwanda last. Also, It is said that Tutsis were Nilotic people who wandered around following the Nile River searching for food for their cattles and ended up in Rwanda. The Tutsis made up to fourteen percent of the citizens of Rwanda.

Twa, Tutsi and Hutu spoke the same language "Kinyarwanda". They lived amicably, shared everything, and had one king "Umwami" that ruled them all. Everyone was the Umwami's subjects and everything in the kingdom belonged to him. Others were mere stewards.

In old Rwanda, cows represented riches. Since Tutsis were herders, Tutsi became synonym of rich. Umwami had the right to make any decision he wanted. So, in favor of Umwami, Hutus could become Tutsis and Tutsis could become Hutus if Tutsis did something wrong to displease Umwami, and he takes away their possessions. Because of all of this, the differences between the Hutu and the Tutsi were insignificant and were more similar to class divisions rather than ethnic divisions. The Rwandan people believed that God visited around the world during the day, but at the end of the day he rested in Rwanda.

During colonization, Rwanda was given to Germany. However, during that time, Germany didn't change much in the country as they thought Rwanda was governing herself well. After Germany committed the crime of genocide against the Jews and lost World War II, its African colonies were divided among European countries. In this split, Rwanda went to Belgium. The Belgians saw how Rwandans were governing themselves and how they were united. They saw it as a threat and decided to put division among Rwandans.

Belgians thought Hutus and Tutsis were different biologically and intellectually and even brought scientists to try to prove this theory with all kinds of tools and measurements. The Hutu people were found to be shorter, darker, with wider and bigger noses than the Tutsi people. The Belgians also believed the Hutus' noses to be about double the size of Tutsis. The Belgians favored the Tutsi people because they believed Tutsis were more similar to Caucasians.

Then, in the 1930s, the Belgians wanted to further standardize the division and introduced Rwandan identity cards, which labeled every Rwandan either as Hutu, Tutsi or Twa. This was the colonizers' way of manipulating the Rwandese and was the sowing of an evil seed whose fruit would later destroy the Rwandan population. Under Belgian colonial rule, Catholics and other religious orders operated the schools, and these schools favored Tutsis at the expense of the Hutus.

Later, Belgian priests who had overcome inferiority in their own country after WWII came over to Rwanda. They sided with the Hutu people and encouraged them to fight for their rights. By this time, colonization was nearly at its end because the United Nations was urging Belgium to get out of Rwanda. At the same time, Hutu activists were demanding their rights as the majority of the population.

Rwandan brothers fought their own, robbed each other, and killed their own people instead of fighting the evil ideologies Europeans planted in their minds. Our beloved country lost the unity and love we once had for each other. That was the beginning of the fallout that ruined our relationships; the love and bond we had for each other got stained by the blood of innocent people.

Chapter 3

"A voice is heard in Ramah, mourning and great weeping, Rachel weeping for her children and refusing to be comforted, because her children are no more."

~ *Jeremiah 31: 15*

The Hutu brother disregarded the conscious his Maker had given him and ignored what he shared with his Tutsi brother, and the love they shared and the bond they had. He didn't realize that hating and killing Tutsi would make him more vulnerable to the enemy. They had forgotten that they were stronger together. The Hutu obeyed the whispers and lies of the colonialist and decided to act on his emotions without thinking to himself *"what's in it for them?"* Then the door was opened wider for the enemies to come in as they pleased and these intruders kept feeding him more lies to keep the two brothers apart. Therefore, the two brothers became enemies and fought over their treasured kingdom, Rwanda.

Violence broke out in 1959, with Hutus killing Tutsis. By this time, government propaganda and colonial administration, and Catholic priests spread inciting information that Tutsis were not Rwandans but were aliens from the Horn of Africa. They were no longer viewed as Rwandese, but were called foreigners who had invaded Rwanda from Ethiopia. They were urged to go back to where they had come from. At this time, Belgians were behind the Hutus, helping them get rid of Tutsis.

———————

I remember my parents used to tell us that in 1959 during the slaughter, a lot of Tutsis were killed or forced to flee the country. But, still, it never occurred to me that there were people out there who couldn't return to Rwanda. It was folklore until it became a reality. My father told us that we had a couple of uncles in Uganda. I remember him going to visit our family there, but then I did not ask why they lived there and why they never visited us.

The killings of 1959 did not greatly affect the area where my father and mother were living. At that time, my parents were a young couple, and they had only a newborn, my eldest brother Nkubili. The Hutu families who were their neighbors were good to them.

However, when the violence erupted, Hutus were obligated to do what the government told them. My parents' neighbors burned down houses but before the neighbors burned down any Tutsi houses they helped them to empty their houses and hid their belongings in their own homes. The Hutus told men to go hide in the mountains with their cattle until things calmed down. The women and children were left behind to hide in the Hutu neighbors' houses.

After the killings, the Hutus helped the Tutsis rebuild their homes and gave them back their belongings. However, in other areas across the country, a lot of Tutsis were killed. Those who escaped the slaughter scattered to different countries around Rwanda. Many settled in Uganda. They tried to come back several times by force but they never succeeded.

The government in Rwanda lived in fear of these large groups that were in exile in surrounding countries. Every time the Tutsis, who were still in exile, attacked the government, the government massacred Tutsis inside Rwanda. However, these acts were never obvious to the average citizen. The government always made it appear as though it was rebels who had killed them. They made sure to cover it up.

The Tutsi refugees in the neighboring countries continued to press the government in Rwanda for a peaceful return but it never happened. They were always told that Rwanda was too full and there was no space for them.

Having been in exile for more than 30 years, some of the Rwandese refugees chose just to forget about ever returning to Rwanda. They started to embrace what they had and build a life where they were.

A friend of mine, Dr. Lonzen Rugira, who was born and grew up in Uganda as a refugee, told me how in Uganda, refugees got very comfortable. Afterward, things changed when Milton Obote, the president of Uganda at the time, did not like the Rwandese. Two young Rwandese developed a close friendship with the rebel leader for the liberation of Uganda, Yoweri Museveni, now president of Uganda. When Obote won the elections in Uganda, Museveni started a rebellion. Among the original soldiers that started the rebellion with Museveni were those two young Rwandese, Fred Rwigema and Paul Kagame, the current president of Rwanda. The rest of the Rwandese young men followed.

The Rwandese involvement in the Ugandan struggle brought many consequences. When Obote became president, he made sure that all Rwandese paid the price. Rwandese were repressed, killed, and thrown off their property. When Museveni later won the war, many soldiers in his force were Rwandese.

By 1990, Rwandese refugees in the National Army of Ugandan formed their own army. They felt they were strong enough to fight for their rights in their own country. A conference was arranged and in the late 1980s, a political movement named the "Rwandese Patriotic Front"

(RPF) was formed to return to their Rwandese home by any means necessary.

PART II: Terror
Chapter 4

"...Tyranny will be far from you; you will have nothing to fear. Terror will be far removed; it will not come near you."

~ *Isaiah 54:14*

Back in Rwanda, the Tutsis were still being treated badly and were being exploited. Tutsi were not allowed to be in more than five percent of the positions in the workplace or in schools. They were not allowed to visit those in exile. Moreover, if they tried secretly, and got caught, they were put in jail or simply killed. By the time the Rwandese Patriotic Front (RPF) formed, people − especially young people—were starting to leave the country to join the refugees of Rwanda.

On October 1, 1990, the RPF army, led by Fred Rwigema, attacked Rwanda. Coming home peacefully was not an option, so they fought intensely for several days. Fred Rwigema lost his life in that war. The army lost the battle, but they never gave up. They did not want to go back to Uganda to be treated like "foreigners," when they had their own country. Tutsis in Rwanda paid the price. Tutsis were massacred in the Northern part of the country. A lot of people were put in jail because they were accused of being RPF accomplices. Regular citizens were treated like enemies of the nation. Many were arbitrarily put in jail, tortured. Most of them were Tutsis hence.

My brother Nkubili was one of them. Not only was he was a Tutsi, he was also a journalist. An intellectual who was using his education and job to promote social justice in a country where people were being excluded for their ethnic background. He worked for the oldest independent paper in the country. Nkubili's home was raided like one of a criminal. I heard that bullet holes were still visible through the doors and wall. He was not home when they came for him and they forced open all the doors.

He never came back home that day and his wife, Anastasia, who had a newborn that was only a few weeks old did not know what to do. She went back and forth to all the places the government was detaining people looking for him. Nkubili was nowhere to be found for months. His wife eventually sent a message home saying that Nkubili might be dead. Since the paper was a private institution, they had stopped his salary. With her small salary, she was struggling to provide for herself and her two small children. Anastasia had to move her family to a smaller, more affordable home.

Eventually the family got word that he was alive. He was being held prisoner with another group of journalists. Like many other Tutsi journalists at that time, he was tortured and starved. I heard that during that time the only thing they were given was water, often being forced to drink it from their shoes.

Nkubili was in jail for six months and there was no trial. Following an outcry from an international human rights organization, he and the other prisoners were released. Nkubili had missed out on the first six months of his youngest daughter's life. He returned to his job but he was never paid for any arrears. Though broken and pained by the rejection of his own country, he stayed and kept fighting for justice. Nkubili even decided to join the opposition by becoming a member of a political party. Up until that point, my brother had never showed an in interest in politics.

Following the RPF attack, everything in the country got out of control. From the time the RPF army attacked to the point when the genocide broke out, the extremists started convincing the general population that the RPF were "devils" and that once they succeeded in their plans to take over the country, they would wipe out all the Hutus. Therefore, the Hutus needed to act fast and first. The extremists convinced the Hutus that ordinary Tutsis were conspiring with the rebels by sending their children to fight. They said all Tutsis were part of the army. Also, they were told all Tutsis were financially supporting the RPF.

The government also brought back the 1959 strategy that Tutsis were foreigners, while they were allies in their country. The "foreigners" needed to be sent back to Ethiopia where they had originated. In fact, the Hutu extremists offered to provide a shortcut to Ethiopia, for the Tutsis, which was the nearest river, where their bodies would float back to their origin.

At that time, Tutsi people were getting killed every day in different locations of the country. As the government killed people, the RPF never gave up either. At the same time, the government of Rwanda was fearful the RPF fighters would continue to advance, they began to negotiate with their enemy to restore peace and share power.

While all these negotiations were taking place, the extremists, with the help of the army, were handing out weapons to gangs that had been trained by the French. The casualties were Tutsis and moderate Hutus. The extremists were finally ready to get rid of the problem, the Tutsis. During this time, they formed a club called "Hutu Power." This club was anti-Tutsi and also against any Hutus who did not accept the 'Hutu Power' ideology. The leader of this new club happened to be an editor at a newly formed radio station. This hate radio station would prove to be instrumental in the spread of the ideology calling for the "clean-up" job. The hate radio station started disseminating hate information.

The worst came when, on April 6th, the president of Rwanda, returning from a conference, was killed when missiles hit his plane. The accident occurred while the pilot was attempting to land at the airport in Kigali. It was said that the plane was crashed by the RPF soldiers and because of it all, the Tutsi had to pay the price for it. As if they had waited for the plane to crash, the militia established roadblocks all over Kigali as soon as the presidential plane went down. The first people targeted were Tutsis and the elite Hutus who had remained moderates. The militia had recruited from the poor, the unemployed, homeless, street youths, and criminals. They received the authority to kill, rape, and steal. In just days, the killing spread all over the country. The Hutus were instructed to kill all Tutsis in order to save their own lives. Overnight, killing Tutsi became a fulltime job.

Chapter 5

"... Fear not, I have redeemed you; I have called you by name, you are mine. When you pass through the waters, I will be with you; and through the rivers, they shall not overwhelm you; when you walk through fire, you shall not be burned, and the flame shall not consume you. For I am the Lord your God, the Holy One of Israel, your Savior...Because you are precious in my eyes, and honored and I love you."

~ Isaiah 43:1-4

As I was growing up, my parents taught us not to hate or disrespect others. So, when the government started encouraging the Hutus to kill us, I wondered if I was hallucinating. How was it that the country I loved, despised me? How could children I grew up with taunt me when they saw me? How did this hatred start? What did I do? What did my people do to be loathed this much? Many questions flooded my mind with no one there to answer them. I felt lost. Regardless of what my father had told me about 1959, I couldn't believe it. Although I knew that I was Tutsi, it never seemed like a big deal because I had grown up with Hutu children. I never thought of them as being different from us.

During the genocide, I wondered why my parents never told us about the extreme hostility that had developed over the years between

Tutsis and Hutus. Before the genocide broke out, I really didn't know or care much about my ethnicity. It wasn't until I saw my parents and family members slaughtered, that I started to experience the fear of being hunted day and night. At that time, I began to truly realize what ethnicity was doing to our country. I could not understand why these people hated us so much that they wanted us killed. There was a roadblock at every corner of the street so people could not escape or hide in neighboring houses. People with machetes, grenades, guns, sticks, axes, dogs and anything that could be used for harm controlled the streets and trails. Tutsis became targets and Hutus had permission to kill and violate them in any way they wanted.

I remember the genocide as if it was yesterday, when the horror that consumed my people broke out. It was during Easter break, right after I came home from visiting my older sister Christina and my niece Gabriella in Butare. I loved to go there and spend time with them. Since my parents lived in the village, it was always nice to go into the city. As everywhere in the world, children love to take exciting news back to school. It is especially true in the village, where people are not exposed to much. Even sharing that where you went on vacation had electricity was amazing to them. Up until this day, there is no electricity in the village where I grew up. When I was growing up, I thought of village life as being boring, but now I long for that period of innocence and the love people had for one another. There was a sense of community, knowing that everyone was watching you no matter what you did or where you were. As a child, you were accountable to your community. You could get punished by any adult, and that adult didn't have to be your relative or even know you. The village where I grew up was the true definition of the saying, "It takes a village to raise a child". They took it literally. Thing are different in the city, where everyone minds their own business. I remember when I was a child I was afraid of doing anything bad, because I knew someone might see me and tell my parents. At the time, I hated it, but now I appreciate the fact I had people to watch over me wherever I was.

But during the genocide, these same neighbors turned against us and used dogs to hunt Tutsis down, as though we were beasts. They mocked and shouted when they saw a Tutsi as if it were a sin to be one. I was confused. How could the whole world watch and do nothing to stop this animosity? Where was humanity? Where was the United Nations? Were we not human or valued enough to be rescued from these people who were possessed by the devil? Where were all the godly people? Were all people around the world blind or deaf to hear that we were being killed and hunted day and night? I believe the churches and the people in Rwanda who called themselves Christians were possessed by the devil, for they too were involved in the killings. People were not even afraid to go into churches to kill people. So-called priests opened the gates so the murderers could get inside. I believe each person has a purpose in life because that's what God tells us. Were we Tutsis born to be killed? That's the question that floats through my mind to this day.

When I was a little girl, I used to dream about what I would be like when I was in my late twenties. I dreamt that I would graduate from school, have a good job and be able to help my parents with everything they ever dreamed of doing. Once my parents were "all set", I would get married. All those girly dreams were shattered in my early teen years. My parents were killed along with four of my siblings, Nkubili, Sesonga, Augustin and Sylvie. Many of the people that I grew up with were killed during the genocide and much of my village is now surrounded by bushes and no people live there.

I thank God every day that I wasn't left alone in this world despite losing more than half of my intimate family. I was lucky to have my wonderful big sister, Christina, and two brothers, Mathias and Jean Damascene survive even though we are separated. My two brothers still live in Rwanda while my sister and I live in the United States; because of this distance, we rarely see them. Still, it is a blessing to know that they are alive. Along with my sister, I have three beautiful nieces.

Chapter 6

"No weapon forged against you will prevail, and you will refute every tongue that accuses you."

~ *Isaiah 54:17*

When the genocide started where I lived in 1994, the first thing they did was burn houses. Before the houses were burned, we sometimes slept outside in the bushes. Women and children would go and sleep in the coffee plantation near my house, which belonged to my uncle. Men would stay awake on watch nearby. I was very confused and never understood why we had to hide when I never saw anyone doing anything wrong. I never understood how people could kill someone because of how they were born. After all, in our case, we never chose to be born as Tutsi. Why were we being persecuted for being who we were?

I couldn't understand how I could be hated when I didn't hate anyone. After several days of not sleeping, I started to see houses in the distance on fire far away from where we lived. My parents and uncles must have known what it meant because they told us to leave the place. My parents, Sesonga, Augustin, Sylvie, and myself; my uncles, aunts, cousins and all the people who had been camping at our house for the last few days took a few things we could carry and then went on top of the mountain near a desolate area. Near the location of our camp, you could still see our home, along with thousands of other abandoned homes of Tutsis who escaped for their lives.

It was Monday the 10th of April in the year 1994, around six in the evening when I saw our house go up in flames. I saw our memory, our dreams, and all the things we cherished in our home, engulfed. In that moment, my father aged right before my eyes. The flames went up high and the smell of smoke and the roof of our house completely burnt to the ground. As the house crumbled down, my father's knee weakened and he sat on the ground.

My mother was in shock. All she did was hold her children by her side. She held us like the end of the world had come and we were going to shatter like glass. As if she could not let go of our hands, not even for a second.

Our parents consoled us, Sylvie and Augustin on either side of our mother, and me sitting in front of her. My brother Sesonga was standing next to my father, emotionless. My uncles, aunts, cousins, and other Tutsis who were at the top of the mountain, all stood watching the blaze of the houses. You could hear howling everywhere.

My family and I stayed there overnight with people I had never seen before. They were Tutsis from all over. All night the men were planning how we would leave in the middle of the night to go to Burundi. Around midnight, my mother told me that I needed to get up because it was time to go. We walked all night and when morning came, we passed burnt and abandoned houses. All along the way, we met other people fleeing their villages. A large group of us walked all day.

When we had almost reached the border of Rwanda and Burundi, I heard screaming, "Don't let them cross!"

Then Hutus, from both sides of the border, surrounded us in a circle and told us to return to our homeland areas. Because our family and the other people who were with us knew that we would be killed if we went back, the men tried to force their way through. However, because they were exhausted and were surrounded, they did not succeed. These Hutu men took many of our possessions from us, including the cattle. The Hutus tried to beat up most of the Tutsi young men who had attempted to push their way past these Hutus who were on guard.

My family and all the Tutsi we were with were told to return to our now ruined homes. We had been robbed of most of everything we had, and some of the men were bleeding from the beatings. Very exhausted from hearing the men make unreasonable demands, my father suggested to us all, "You know, let's go home. Nothing will happen; if we do what they are suggesting, I don't think they will kill us."

Eventually, we had to turn around and go back because we had no other choice. Our parents were hoping to be given mercy by the neighbors they had grown up and shared everything with for as long as they could remember. They didn't realize that the generation that saved their lives back in 1959 was now gone. The new generation that had emerged was bloodthirsty, greedy and did not care about anyone.

We walked all the way back to where we used to live. As we neared our home, Hutus from a different location saw us first, and began yelling, "The Tutsis are coming back."

Everyone heard; even the ones who were inside their houses came outside. By the time we reached the ruins of our house, we saw many people running toward us. They were screaming and carrying machetes, knives, sticks and nail-spiked clubs. It was then that I understood— we were about to be killed. The devastating thing was that those people coming toward us were our neighbors, the very people I grew up with, families I had shared meals with, children I had played with, and people I had known all my life. I couldn't understand how people could turn against us in such a short period of time.

I looked at my parents. The only thing I saw was despair, which caused me to realize how hopeless things had become. How could these people greet us with machetes and grenades? I watched, helpless, as they beat up our brothers and parents in front of our eyes.

That day, they were not touching women and little children, yet. I remember some young men running and a crowd of people ran after them and killed them. The older people, who didn't have strength, like my father, women, and children, sat there motionless and waited to be massacred. I also remember seeing this young man I had known all my life holding a knife to the throat of another man who was sitting still, scared, sick, and hungry because he hadn't eaten for days. He was just sitting there. This young man in his early twenties began yelling and daring him to move an inch and see how his throat would be cut into pieces. He sat there like he did not even exist anymore. He looked as if he didn't even care about dying, as if living was misery enough. Everything had begun to terrify me and seeing this man do this caused me to be even more petrified; I looked at my mother and decided that I had to run. I don't even think I had thought through the implications of what I was going to do; the only thing that ran through my head was to run for my life. As I think back now, I know if it hadn't been God's plan for me to live, I would have died that day. Every time someone ran, people chased and killed them instantly.

Before I decided to run for my life, I had my cousin's baby, Clarisse, with me. From the time when my family fled our home, Clarisse had been by my side and never left me except upon occasion when I became tired and her father carry her to give me a little relief. I can never forget about this little girl because Clarisse's death has haunted me for a long time, wondering why I never took her with me. This little girl loved me so much. I was the only one who could soothe her when she was crying. The love between me and this little girl was a mystery. Clarisse used to sleep at my house when she was less than a year old and her mother was still nursing her. And when she learned how to crawl, her mother found her trying to crawl to my house. I remember when I used to come home from school, and if she heard my voice… no matter what she was doing, whether she was eating or bathing, she would come running to see me. I loved her so much. There was not a day that passed without us seeing each other. And if I went somewhere for a couple days, I couldn't wait to come back to see Clarisse. I always brought her something back. So, when people were coming to kill us, I had her in my arms. Clarisse's mother was caring for a week-old baby; when the genocide broke out, she was still on bedrest so I was trying to keep Clarisse occupied for her. Clarisse's mom was still weak and could not even walk. Thus, when all the commotion was happening, I couldn't bear the thought of this little one dying in my hands. I went to Clarisse's father and said, "Here is your child, I don't want her to get killed with me." After I handed that baby to my cousin, I ran.

When my mother saw me running, she called me to come back, but I didn't even turn around, I just continued running as fast as possible. I didn't stop and was not even certain where I was going toward. Up to this day, I can still hear my mother calling my name to come back. Sometimes, I wish I had said goodbye to my mother before I left. There was no way to know that minute would be the last time I would see her or hear her beautiful voice calling my name.

After running quite a distance, I finally arrived at my Hutu neighbor's house. The lady who lived there was my mother's goddaughter named Emilienne. When I arrived, Emilienne was sitting outside. The minute she saw me, she was terrified for me because she was unsure if I was being followed or if anyone had seen me entering the house. Emilienne urged me to go quickly and hide in the house. She was so sad and wished that there was a way she could save my mother. Emilienne told me that she would do anything she could to hide me and that the least she could do was to save one of Verediane's children. I lived there, but each day was dreadful. I couldn't go outside or talk because every day the violence got worse.

Luckily, no one knew that I was there; until one day, Emilienne's step-daughter-in-law walked in unannounced. Emilienne never had any children of her own; however, her husband had children from his first marriage. When Emilienne married this man, she was older and had a lot of money. Her stepchildren were always envious of her even though she was nice to them and loved her stepchildren and their children.

I was sitting inside the house, a hut with only three rooms. The first room was the one you see standing from outside the house, similar to a hallway. The other room was round in the middle, which is where they sat at night to have dinner — that's also where the kitchen was. The other room had their bed in it and at the bottom of the bed was where they stored their belongings. Most of the time, I sat on their bed or if they thought someone might come to find me, I'd sit between these big pots on the bottom of their bed. There were times when I hid between things that were stored under their bed.

When Emilienne's step-daughter-in-law came into the house, I was sitting in the middle of the room because I didn't expect anyone to come inside. Their house didn't have a room I could easily escape to. I tried to escape under the bed; but I didn't have enough time to slide in there. Seeing her standing there, I knew my life was over.

After Emilienne's step-daughter-in-law saw me she jumped too, because she was not expecting anyone to be there. She said a fake hello and then left. After a little while, when Emilienne came back home, I told her what had happened. She spoke to her husband, who went and pleaded with his daughter-in-law never to tell anyone that I was there. The daughter-in-law told her father-in-law that she didn't understand why her in-laws were hiding a cockroach. This was the name they were using to describe Tutsis at that time. She promised her father-in-law that she would never tell anyone.

However, after a couple of weeks of living there, Emilienne's step-daughter-in-law started threatening to tell others that I was there. Emilienne and her husband thought it was all talk and never thought she would actually do it. In the beginning of the genocide they were not killing women and children that much. When Hutus caught women and children, they rounded them up as prisoners and guarded them to watch for anyone bringing water or food to them. Because of this, Emilienne and her husband were not worried much about her threats. They just told me to ignore her nonsense, and believed that she would not tell anyone.

While I was living at Emilienne's, I heard that my mother, my aunts and cousins, were still alive being held nearby. No one was supposed to bring them anything. Every night Emilienne would cry and tell me that she wished there was a way to bring my mother food or water. My little brother, Augustin, and sister, Sylvie, were there too, but at that point, there was no way I could get to them. There were roadblocks and guards at every corner.

By this time, my father was dead. He had been killed the same day I had run to Emilienne's house. That day, they took the older men, like my father, who couldn't get away and placed them together in a field. These men were then bombarded with grenades. The ones that didn't die were cut into pieces or beaten to death. That day, one of my uncles was sliced across his throat when he got up to try and fight, because the grenade didn't finish him.

All the time that I had been living at Emilienne's house, I had known that my father had been killed. He died on Wednesday, April 13, 1994, a day I will never forget. At the point of my father's death, I was glad that he was out of his misery. He was better off getting killed by a grenade. I hoped that the grenade had hit him, causing him to die instantly. This type of death seemed quicker than him being tortured like those who had been cut into pieces or beaten to death. I also had heard that my brother Sesonga was still alive and was hiding in the nearby mountains.

For a while, I felt guilty knowing that I had food and shelter while my mother and my siblings who remained alive were living outside, in the pouring rain with nothing to eat. It sickened my heart.

Eventually, I received word that Clarisse's little baby sibling had died because her mother no longer had anything to feed her as she was too sick to produce milk. I couldn't imagine what it must been like to have her baby die in front of her, and being powerless to do anything about it.

To this day, I wonder where Clarisse's mom put her after she died. She was closed up inside that place, with only starved children and their mothers who were powerless to help her, themselves or even their own children. Her husband was not even there anymore. I had heard that after Clarisse's little sibling died, her mother tried to put Clarisse back on breast milk because she didn't have anything else to give her. However, in the end, Clarisse died in her mother's arms as well. There couldn't have been much left in her breasts because she, herself, was getting no water or food.

After the genocide, I couldn't look any child in the eye; I felt so guilty and regretted leaving that child. I could not explain to myself why I didn't run with Clarisse or carry her with me. For a very long time, I was tormented because every time I saw a baby who resembled Clarisse l broke down and cried. For a long time, I was afraid to allow myself to become attached to a child. I became convinced that if I loved a child, that the child would die.

After living at Emilienne's house for a while, I lost track of the days and was unable to tell one from the other; a day seemed like a week and week felt like a month. On a day that I remember like it was yesterday, it was in the middle of the afternoon, I heard the commotions of roaring guns, grenades and screaming. At that moment nobody needed to tell me anything. I knew they were killing my family; my mom, my siblings, and my cousins. I don't know how I can explain it but I felt so connected to my family in that moment. I don't know if the fear that gripped my mother and siblings transferred to me in their final moments or if it was God's innate power at work. That day, a piece of me died with them even though I was alive. I didn't want to hide any longer. Instead, I wished I'd never ran away, I wished I had died with them. What I was feeling was worse than dying. I didn't cry. There didn't seem to be any point of living anymore without any parents or my siblings. From that day forward, I stopped being afraid of death. I just wanted to die and go to be with family. I was physically alive but a part of me had died that day. The thought of knowing that my mother was lying on the ground dead and undignified haunted me.

Up to this day, I do not understand why my life was spared. All I know, is that it was not the Hutus who wanted me alive, neither was I better than anyone else. All I know in my heart of all hearts, God had a bigger plan for me and had saved my life for that very reason. I may sometimes not understand or know why I was spared; still, I should trust and believe that He knows better that I am alive and caring for myself and those who surround their lives with mine.

God's word says, "As the Heavens is higher than the Earth, so are my ways higher than your ways and my thoughts higher than your thoughts." (Isaiah 55:9)

All I know is my Redeemer lives and My God did not protect me in vain. There is a reason.

Chapter 7

"Even though I walk through the valley of shadow of death, I will fear no evil, for you are with me, your rod and your staff, they comfort me. You prepare a table before me in the presence of my enemies. You anoint my head with oil; my cup overflows. Surely goodness and love will follow me all the days of my life."

~ Psalms 23:4-6

When Emilienne came home that night, she was heartbroken as she broke the news of my family's death to me. She didn't have to tell me anything, because in my heart, I knew. For nearly a month, I stayed in her home until one day her stepdaughter-in-law told people that I was still alive. Shortly after the news about me spread, Isaiah, one of my former neighbors, came to the house. No one was home except the little children. I could hear him outside asking the kids to get me and bring me outside. The children told him that I was not there. He called my name a couple of times and told me that I should come out and go with him. Isaiah said he was not going to do anything to me except take me to his house to hide me. I ignored him because I knew he was not going to come in the house without permission. He was there for a while, but gave up and left. I was relieved.

The next morning, however, Isaiah came back with a gang of people shouting and chanting evil songs. You could hear them miles away before they reached the house. Emilienne and her husband panicked and told me to go hide in a hole that they made banana wine in, which was in their backyard. As the chanting got closer, Emilienne and her husband panicked. Then, in a couple of minutes, Emilienne came back and told me that the killers would find me, and she couldn't bear to see me killed in front of her. She told me to run to her stepson's house until the gang of people left.

Sometimes when the people who were killing came to your house and found that you were harboring a Tutsi there, they would make you kill the person you were hiding and would order you to bury them as well. And if someone in the home refused to follow orders, they then killed everybody in that home. I think Emilienne and her husband were afraid of that. I don't blame them. They did everything possible to protect me. Whatever was going to happen was out of their control. My fate was in God's hands.

The day I fled from Emilienne's house, it was pouring rain. I was barefoot and wearing a skirt that you wrap around your waist. The skirt was one that my sister had bought me when I was at her house during a vacation. I also had on an oversized sweater, which was used to cover my head to shelter from the rain and to hide my face from the people I passed. I remember being grateful that I had something with which to cover my head. I ran as fast as possible, but I didn't succeed because halfway there, Isaiah caught me. I guess they went to the house, searched for me, and when they didn't find me, the bloodthirsty men followed my footprints in the mud. When Isaiah saw me, he yelled for me to stop right there. Knowing what would happen if I chose to disobey, I stopped. I didn't see the point of running.

At that time, I didn't care anymore. I just wanted to die. I asked God to take my soul and hoped that they would not torture me. Isaiah took me and told me that my life was over. He said that if I would have gone with him the night before, I would have been saved and that it was my fault. For some reason, at this point, I was not even scared. I just listened to him and didn't say a word. I felt that if it was my time to go, then let it be. After all, my whole family had been slaughtered, and what was the use of struggling everyday, thinking about tomorrow? I never wanted to die more than I did that day. I was kind of glad that I was going to be reunited with my family, even if it was in death.

Isaiah, and the other people with him, took me a few miles from where I was hiding. We met other murderers who were going around searching for people to kill. They had gathered little children who they had uncovered from different hideouts. The people who had become murderers were beating the children with belts and sticks, calling them snakes and cockroaches. They said that they should kill them because Paul Kagame and Fred Rwigema, the Tutsi rebel leaders, had left when they were young and then returned as soldiers. They went on to say that when you let a snake live without killing it and its young ones, eventually, the snake grows and comes to bite you.

Chapter 8

"For I am the Lord your God, who takes hold of your right hand and says to you do not fear; I will help you. Do not be afraid, O worm [Anamaliya], O little [Anamaliya], for I myself will help you, declares the Lord, your redeemer the Holy One of Israel."

~ Isaiah 41:13-14.

Isaiah and his co-murderers took me and the children away. Isaiah was a high school student probably in his late teens. And as I said before, we were neighbors. We had a history of some sorts. One day when he was on school vacation, I passed his house. When Isaiah saw me that day, he asked me if he could walk me home. At that time, long before the genocide, I was very shy around boys. However, because I knew him from growing up together, I agreed to let him walk me home. On the way to my house, Isaiah asked me if we could sleep together. I couldn't believe him. I looked at him, burst out laughing, and left him standing there while I ran home. Thinking about it now, I suppose I humiliated him, but as a teenager I didn't care or really think much about it. After that incident, every time Isaiah saw me, he would give me a dirty look and told me that I was mean. I forgot all about the incident until that day during the genocide when they came to get me. I realized then that Isaiah still had a grudge against me because I didn't agree to sleep with him.

While they were debating whether to kill me or not, someone said, "Don't kill her. She is a young girl and is not going to grow up to do anything. Besides, her parents were really nice people; why can't someone take her and make her a wife?" Isaiah responded quickly, "I don't care if you kill all the women, as well. They never wanted to sleep with me anyway. Besides, once I asked her if she would sleep with me and she refused so, I want her to be killed."

Someone in the crowd shouted, "Why can't you have her now? You could do whatever you want. Now, she is all yours."

I was terrified not just by the thought of being killed, but also by the thought of being raped. I prayed in my mind that I would die and go unite with my family who had deceased. I also asked God to protect me from being raped. The thought of it made me nauseous.

Luckily, among the group of people taking innocent lives was my cousin's husband Tim and Colonel, a guy I knew who used to be one of my best friend's friend. I hate to admit it, but Colonel is the one who saved my life that time, even though he is the one who killed my father and my uncles by throwing grenades at them. I now understand when the Bible says that sometimes God uses evil people to do good things for the sake of His people. I knew Colonel was going around killing innocent people. When I saw him, he was wearing grenades and had a bayonet in his hand. I think that even the people who were committing murderous acts were afraid of him. Colonel's whole family was involved in the genocide. At that time, Colonel spoke, "No one is killing Anamaliya. She is going to be Rutindo's wife." Isaiah went out of control and said that he was the one who knew where I was. He demanded to be the one to take me home. Then Colonel stepped in and put a bayonet to his throat. Colonel told Isaiah that he would kill him that instant if he kept running his mouth. In my mind, I kept considering which choice was worse, dying or becoming the wife of that Rutindo.

Rutindo was a nasty old man. Since I was a child he had looked the same, ragged, and dirty. He had never married and people said that he was impotent. Every time I had seen him, he was either drunk, or yelling and fighting with people. I felt so disgusted inside I just wanted to die instead of going to be his wife. At that moment, Tim, my cousin's husband, came and whispered into my ear that this was just a way of saving my life. I wasn't actually expected to become Rutindo's wife. Then I felt relief. Later, I found out that Tim was the one who begged Colonel to save my life.

Among the crowd was Rutindo's little brother, who was probably in his late twenties. He took me to their mother's house, because Tim didn't want to show he was involved in the plan to save me. When I got there, two of Rutindo's sisters were at the house. One of his sisters was so nice to me that she helped me a lot by encouraging me and telling me that everything would be okay. But the other sister didn't seem to care about what was happening. She always looked angry and scary. I stayed there for about two weeks. During my time there, my cousin Alexia, Tim's wife, came to visit me. They were neighbors. Alexia told me that my Aunt Felecite, her mother, was still alive and was at her house. I was glad to hear that another one of my family members was alive.

After a couple of days, even the evil Colonel came to see us. He said that since he saved my life, I was going to repay him when I grew up. Who knows what he meant by that? I stayed there for a while, since they lived in the center of everything. Everyone knew that I was still alive. A few weeks later, Rutindo went wild and said he wanted his wife since I had been given to him in order not to die. Then my nightmare truly began. Every day he was complaining about me not being with his wife. Since he didn't live with his mother, I heard all this from the people around me.

One day when everyone was gone except for his mother and me, Rutindo became very drunk. He sent this boy, one of their neighbors, to come and get me. "Rutindo and the chief of the soldiers told me to come get you and he wants you to be his wife or you will be killed," the boy said. The first time I said 'no' he left without me. I was afraid of going outside. It was unheard of for a Tutsis to be seen outside unless you were going to be killed. Fifteen minutes later, the boy came back and said that the chief's soldiers - said to choose between being a wife, or dying. Since my family had been slaughtered, I didn't see any reason for living. I told this boy that I would rather be killed than be Rutindo's wife.

Meanwhile, Rutindo's mother was on the sideline observing and listening to what was happening. She didn't say anything the whole time. When she heard me saying that I would choose death rather than being her son's wife, she spoke up by saying, "You know there is nothing wrong with being a wife." She also stated, "Have you gotten your period anyway?" I lied and said that I hadn't, thinking she would feel sorry for me and tell her son that I was still too young. This was half-true, because how could a teenager who hadn't even discovered herself—plus a child who had lost her whole family and was also fighting for her life, be a wife to anyone, let alone to a nasty old man.

After Rutindo's mother told me it was better to be Rutindo's wife than to die, I didn't respond because she didn't understand the situation I was in; but, then, how could she? All my family had died horrible deaths, and here I was all by myself in a world filled with enemies wanting to kill me. All his mother cared about was finding a wife for her old nasty son.

Forget about this sick man wanting to marry a barely teenage girl, even if I was mature and old enough to marry, I couldn't imagine marrying this man and having Hutu children, after all they had done to my family. In Rwanda, the children belong to the husband's side of the family, which means the ethnicity of the children is determined by the man. So, there was no way in the world I was going to do that. When the boy came to take me the second time, I was gladly willing to be killed. Now, there was no point of living anymore. What was I living for, anyway? Nonetheless, I followed him. When we got a little distance from Rutindo's mother's house, we met one of his sisters coming home.

When she saw me, she was horrified. She couldn't believe that I would go outside. She asked what I was doing and insisted that I go back inside before someone else saw me. I told her where I was going. She told me to hurry and return to the safety of the house. Also, she told me if they want to come and kill me, they should come to me instead of me giving them the pleasure of going to them. I went back inside as I was instructed. When we got home, she was so mad at her mother. "How could you let her go?" She asked. Her mother insisted there was nothing she could do if they wanted to take me.

Rutindo's sister stayed with me for a while to see if there was anyone else coming to get me. After waiting for few hours, nobody came. Rutindo's sister told me that he was a coward and probably making all that up. Nobody was ordering him to come and get me. Eventually, his sister told me she needed to go see someone and advised me not to leave the house no matter what. After she left, the messenger boy came again as though he had been waiting for her to leave. He said Rutindo was mad, and he wanted me to come right way. He told me that this time he was not going without me, because he didn't want to get himself in trouble. By that time, I didn't care anymore. I had had enough. I followed him again.

However, on our way, I realized that we were not going the same way we went the first time. We were walking between houses, as though we were hiding. I didn't care though I just kept following him without asking any questions. Then when we entered one of the houses, I became suspicious. I didn't understand how 'going to be killed' could end us up in a house. A house that belonged to one of the Tutsis men who had been killed. That's how low Rutindo was. He didn't even own his own house. Instead he was happy to take over what was not his. Before the genocide, he didn't own anything, and he lived with his mother. Now, he had ideas of making me a wife in the house that once belonged to one of my family's friends.

When we walked through the door, I saw Rutindo and other men like him. There were no soldiers in sight. So, I sat there and listened to him telling me how he was not going to do anything bad to me. Besides, Rutindo inferred that by making me his wife, he was doing me a favor. My marrying him would spare my life. He insisted this was not what he wanted. It was people pressuring him to do it because I was hiding at their house. Otherwise, he was going to get in trouble himself if he didn't marry me soon. I sat there for probably an hour listening to his stupid excuses for his actions. I didn't say a word. Instead, I was just sitting there like a statue. While I was there, Rutindo's sister and his little brother had returned home. When they didn't find me, they got mad at their mother for letting me go.

Rutindo's sister and brother asked their mother where he had taken me. She told them she didn't know. They knew where he was living and came bursting in the house, yelling at him, and telling him how he should be ashamed of himself and if he cared about getting married why he couldn't find someone his own age, instead of taking advantage of a child.

Rutindo's brother signaled me to get up and go back home. Then he escorted me back to the house. When I was going back, I was thankful that they didn't come too late and I also was thinking how Rutindo was fighting over me like he owned me, as though I was going to cure an impotent man. This man was over forty years old, never had a girlfriend or even shown interest in women. However, this time he was fighting so hard to force a traumatized teenager to marry him.

When we returned to Rutindo's mother's house, Rutindo's younger brother told me to go and stay at his house with his sister.

The night I stayed with Rutindo's little brother and his sister. Rutindo's younger brother said, "If marrying you will save your life, I would rather do that than let you be my older brother's wife." He said all this and genuinely wanted to do it, but I didn't want to be married to him, either. I had to wonder what was wrong with these people. I didn't want either of them, old or young. It wasn't because I was too young, but mainly because of the thought of knowing I was going to live alone with these animals who had slaughtered all my family and my friends was too much for me to bear.

Next, Rutindo's sister came to my rescue. She said, "No one is marrying her. Can't you people see how young and vulnerable she is?" They guarded me all night. She told me early the next morning to go and live with my cousin Alexia and her husband Tim. She mentioned that Rutindo would be afraid to go there and harass me. Also, she said that she had already talked to them and they agreed to have me there.

Early the next morning, she took me to my cousin Alexia's house. Tim and Alexia lived a couple of houses over from them. When I got there, I saw Alexia's mom, Felecite, for the first time in months. She started to cry when she saw me. I couldn't believe what I saw. Felecite was just skin and bones. She told me on the day we were forced to come back when we were trying to go to Burundi, how they had killed her husband and my father in front of her eyes. Alexia, her daughter, was there as well watching and going crazy, begging them not to kill our family members. She asked them if she could take them to her house. They refused, and instead, murdered all the men that day and told her that she could only take her mother.

When Felecite saw me, it was a reminder of her sadness. She cried so much for my mother and all our family. Felecite told me they killed Verediane, my mother, Sylvie, my little sister, and Augustin, my little brother. Felecite thanked God that I was still alive but wished she didn't have to be alone. I told her that there was nothing she could have done except now sit there and wait for her time. Felecite wished that she had died also, which was exactly how I felt every day. During the genocide, a person who was still alive felt that the dead ones were better off. Living in horror every day, and thinking that tomorrow could or would be your day, was worse because hiding and running was tiring.

The day after I moved into my cousin's house, I heard that, that night Rutindo went to his mother's house, throwing rocks, yelling, and telling them he wanted his wife. He was screaming and demanding that if he didn't get her, he would make them pay. That whole night no one slept. However, after that incident, that was the end of the Rutindo saga. I never heard from him again. A couple of times, he passed by my cousin's house; sometimes, he would come in to sit and talk to Tim. Sometimes, he saw me, but he never said anything to me. I guess he had given up and had come to his senses.

I lived with Tim and Alexia for about a month, I believe this time might have been at the end of May; every night thinking that we could be killed at any moment. As the days went by, my aunt Felecite got so depressed that she couldn't give herself a bath. Felecite was so weak that I had to help take care of her. The first time I helped her with her bath I wanted to cry. You could feel her tailbone sticking out. I think she had given up and wanted to die. Now when I think about it, the people who killed her wasted their time. The condition she was in was early death. I stayed with her, and every day we lived in fear. Some days we were definitely thinking that by nighttime we were going to be killed, while on other nights we didn't think about it.

I came to realize that I didn't even know what day it was. Every day seemed like a hundred days. And, because of living in the house without being able to go outside, I didn't know anything. Every day we spent living was survival. By the middle of May, almost all the people in my town had been killed, including those who had hid in the bushes. Some came out by themselves because of hunger or fatigue from hiding and being hunted down every day. Now, people who were still alive were like me and Felecite, they were hiding in houses. Those who stayed alive were mostly women. No men or little boys were still alive because males no matter how old they were had been considered a threat. These people who were kept alive were considered not to be harmful because they were older women, little girls, and some young women whom Hutu men forced to be their wives. After about two and a half months of killing people night and day, they ran out of jobs. The killers were running out of the excitement they once had for killing and hunting Tutsis in the bushes. There wasn't much to do anymore. Therefore, they needed something to do to entertain themselves.

The murderers decided to go dig in people's houses to see what they could find, and soon their focus shifted to little children and old people.

During the genocide, people who were very old and couldn't get out were burned in their homes. Women who were pregnant had their stomachs cut open, while the killers told them they were making things easier and faster for them. As soon as the torture was complete, they left these women to die. They were not afraid to take women, young or old, even nuns, and rape them. They said that they wanted to know how Tutsi women tasted. Sometimes when they were done raping them they would stick long sticks inside them and would leave them there to die. There was a lot of cruelty out there that is sometimes hard to imagine how any of us that made it out alive.

Two of my cousins were gang-raped, and after the rapists were done, they decided to bury them with half their bodies in the ground and left their heads on top. The dead women were there for days with neighbor's children throwing rocks at them. Days later, one died, and the other one survived. I still don't understand how the one woman survived. After the genocide, when I looked at her, I couldn't even dare to ask what had happened to them or how she felt about everything. I felt even though I had lost everything and was constantly on the run, even emotionally damaged and having come close to death a number of times, I had an easier time in the nightmare compared to hers. It was unimaginable to think of all that she had endured.

Chapter 9

"For I know the plans I have for you,"
declares the Lord, "plans to prosper you and not
to harm you, plans to give you hope and a
future."

~Jeremiah 29:11

Nevertheless, after all these days of living in fear, one-day Tim came home so scared he was convinced that this was the night that we would die. "They are coming to kill you guys," he said. Tim told me to put on some clothes to disguise myself because he was taking me somewhere else.

I didn't want to go because there didn't seem to be a point of always running when eventually I was going to die. I told him that I didn't want to go and that I wanted to die with my aunt Felecite.

Felecite begged me to go and told me that I was still too young to die, and if I went with Tim, maybe I could survive. I wondered what the use of surviving was when there was no one left. She cried and begged me to go. When I saw how she was feeling, how important it seemed to her and the condition she was in, I decided to go with Tim. It was not because I wanted to live but because I didn't want to put Felecite through any more agony.

After changing clothes, I followed Tim. When reached what appeared to be the middle of nowhere, he pulled out a machete and told me that because he had been trying so hard to save my life I should repay him by sleeping with him. He thought that it was the least I could do. Here was my nightmare again. I couldn't believe what he was saying. Of all people, he should have been the last person to think about that. First, Tim was my cousin's husband, and second, he knew the condition I was in better than almost anyone. Tim should have had a little sympathy for me. But then again, who was I to think this now? The continuous lesson was to learn that no one cared what happened to us Tutsis.

At this time Tim was very drunk, which didn't help the situation. I said, "You know what? You are too drunk, so I will pretend that I didn't hear what you said." Hoping he would leave me alone, I kept walking ahead of him. No such luck - Tim became violent. I remember I was wearing a khaki skirt. He threw me on the ground, pulled my skirt up and then cut my underwear into pieces with his machete. I was not scared of him, which gave me the strength to fight. We fought and I didn't give up. He pulled his pants down, and we kept fighting for probably a good thirty minutes. Since Tim was so drunk and didn't have as strong mobility, he eventually got tired and gave up without carrying out his evil plans. He told me that one of these days I would pay for what I did to him. Tim looked humiliated, but pulled up his pants and ordered me to follow him. As horrified as I was walking behind him, I kept thinking how his manly parts were so little. I couldn't imagine how he could get my cousin pregnant, since she was a very tall woman and her husband was a short guy with very small private parts. It looked about the size of a little boy. I really wanted to crack up. I guess it shows how little I knew at that time about how women get pregnant. After that, all the way he was complaining to everyone he passed by about how I was so ungrateful.

It is my opinion that during this period of history no one living in Rwanda had any sense of morals. Usually people would have been ashamed to do what he did, let alone tell people about it. But Tim had no remorse and shared the incident as he passed people on the street.

The sad thing was that not one person rebuked him. People were laughing as though it were funny. Through all this, I continued to follow him, even though I didn't know where he was taking me. Then, after a little while, he told me that I was going to have to live with a friend of his from a Twa (pygmy) family. He said that no one would be able to detect I was hiding there. When we were about to get there, he told me that the pygmy's name was Bubba and that he had known him for a while.

When we arrived, I thought Tim had forgotten about what had happened on our way there. He told Bubba how he asked me to have sex with him and I refused. Then he said, "I would like to see if you could get out of Bubba's hand." At that time, I felt that Tim had just given Bubba permission to do whatever he wanted to me, instead of telling him to protect me. After he said that, Bubba laughed. It was not the kind of laugh you give when something is funny. It was an evil laugh, a laugh that was filled with contempt for another person.

I knew my life was continuously in danger, and at that point, I figured it was time for me to be prepare for anything. Tim left Bubba's, and I stayed there thinking how I would not be in this house if it were not for the genocide.

Where I lived, most people looked at pygmies as low people. Nobody ever went to see them. They were outcasts who lived in isolated places. It was not that people hated them, but they thought of them as dirty people who did not practice hygiene or do things according to societal norms. They lived in their own community governed by their own rules. They married among one another, and most of their marriages were incestuous.

Chapter 10

"Weeping may remain for a night, but rejoicing comes in the morning."

~ Psalms 30:5

Before the genocide, we had a lot of Twas that used to come to our house. They loved my mother, and my mother loved them. They used to visit and bring my mother gifts of beautiful pots. Many people in the village cooked in clay pots, and my mother was fond of them, so she owned many of them. My father used to tease her and often asked her what she planned to do with such a large collection of pots. One thing my mother used her pots for was to make and store a traditional sorghum beer, called ikigage.

We always had ikigage in our house. So when visitors came over, we always had something to give them. It's a Rwandan custom to feed guests and give them your best crops and meats. When the Twas used to come over my mother would load them with lots food and goods to take home. Twas were well known for their ability to dance and my mother loved how they would dance and sing for her during their visits.

When I arrived at Bubba's house, he informed me that he remembered my mother and that she had been the most beautiful and kindest person he had ever known. Bubba said he didn't understand how anyone could kill her. Bubba kept going on and on about Hutus, saying, "Hutus are making big mistakes and whatever they are doing will come back to them." He continued to say that the people who were wonderful and generous to them had been killed, and he wondered how they would now live with the greedy people who had never helped them.

I knew he was killing people, too. I kept thinking how he was like the murderers. How could he condemn other people? How hypocritical was he? Wisely, I just kept my mouth shut. To make matters worse, Bubba was wearing my father's shirt… one which he probably took off of my father's body after he was killed. His son was wearing my brother, Sesonga,' sweater and that was the very sweater Sesonga had been wearing the day we got separated. Just hearing Bubba talk about these things and then seeing him in my dead family's clothes was heartbreaking.

I remember the same day they took me out of Emilienne's house I heard that my brother Sesonga had been found hiding out in the bushes near where we used to live, and then later he had been killed there. I also remember seeing Bubba's son in that mob of people who took me out of Emilienne's house. I couldn't imagine how my brother had spent weeks in the bushes with no food. When I heard the news of him being killed, I didn't even react to it. Sooner, or later, I knew that would be my destiny as well. I just prayed and hoped that he went to heaven with my other family members. Consequently, living at Bubba's house and seeing his son wearing my brother's sweater, I felt as if I were betraying my brother by living with our family's enemies.

After my cousin's husband Tim left me at Bubba's house, I lived there for a little over week. Then, I think Bubba and my cousin's husband Tim began spending time with a lot of people and those people started to suspect where I was once they found out that I had disappeared from Tim's house. They threatened to come to Bubba's house to see if I was there. Bubba told Tim that I had to go somewhere else because he was scared. So, one night Tim and Bubba came together and told me that I had to leave my location because people were coming that night to see if I was hiding there.

The good thing about the men who were killing people, is that most of the time, they announced the impending deaths ahead of time. This often gave people a chance to hide somewhere else before they arrived.

That night we left and walked about an hour before we arrived at my new destination, which was an isolated house at the bottom of a mountain. I couldn't imagine how anyone would have known someone lived there. No other people lived in the vicinity except this old lady and her two sons, who had built their houses around hers. After I saw their place, I thought that this was my survival. No one would ever think to look for me there. They told me that I could probably live in that house for a long time because no one would ever find me there.

Tim and Bubba left me with the old lady, whose name was Madame Zozo. She insisted that her house, which went all the way up to the top of the mountain and down to the bottom, was protected by some type of higher force. She was peculiar, and I sensed there was something going on, even though I didn't know what it was. She took some water and leaves and went around her house, spraying them on the structure. Honestly, I didn't understand what was wrong with her or what she was doing, but I knew there was something strange about her.

Before I found out that she was a psychic she had told me to always stay inside one of the rooms in her house because she had visitors coming to see her daily. At the time, I didn't comprehend what the woman was saying. She did warn me that among those visitors there could be someone who might know me because the they came from everywhere.

Early the next day, visitors came. To my surprise, I knew a couple of the ladies. Even though she told me never to move from the room where I was supposed to hide, my curiosity got the best of me. I got up and peeked through the little hole in the door to see what was happening. I saw these ladies sitting in the circle staring at this old woman as if their lives depended on her.

Sometimes, I wanted to laugh. How could people be so gullible? Even though I was living the last days of my life, I was not dumb enough to come seek answers about the future from this old lady, who claimed to have divine answers for their questions. Some people came and asked if their children were alive, or if the situation they were in would be over soon.

One woman thought her husband was cheating on her. She had come to ask the psychic if her feelings were true. Another woman asked my new landlord if her son was okay where he was living. The old lady responded, "Oh, I can see your son. He is having fun with his friend, and he is laughing." The women were so happy, and thanked the old lady. Then they paid for the answers and good news she gave them. From where I was sitting, I wondered how these women could be so naive. How could their children be 'having fun', as the old lady claimed, in the midst of war and suffering?

I couldn't understand why these women would believe Madame Zozo's responses to their inquiries and be satisfied by the answer, "Your children are happy and are having fun." How could they have fun? Our country was living in the darkest time of our history. Whether you were being killed or just a bystander, it was not a happy time unless you were a perpetrator. I thought those people were foolish and that I had to be the only sane one left, although I was the one being hunted day and night. I felt that the people who were doing the killing no longer had a human spirit. These murderers no longer looked like human beings; they looked like possessed demons. That's why it was so easy for them to hack pregnant women and babies and then repeat these heinous acts repeatedly with no remorse.

During the two weeks I was there with Madame Zozo watching over me, she told me what my future held as well. She told me that my sister Christina was alive, but very sad. Then she told me that if it were not for the situation we were in, Christina would go on to make me rich. After she told me that, I thought what kind of psychic is this? Of course, Christina is sad. Our whole family was gone, and my sister was not safe either. Prior to this conversation, she has asked me if I thought there was anyone in my family still living. I told her that I didn't think so. However, I told her that I have a sister who was married to a Hutu, and I hoped she was still alive. Then, after that she told me all those things about my sister. She probably concluded that since my brother-in-law was a Hutu, she must be alive.

About my sister making me rich, I haven't seen it yet. I am still waiting after twenty years; I don't know when my wealth will come. When I told my sister, and asked her when she was going to make me rich, she answered, "I brought you here to the USA, paid for your ticket, and raised you. What else do you want? As far as I am concerned, it's up to you to become rich. The richness is in your hands. And if you blow it, don't blame me or the poor psychic lady."

The psychic lady was half-right when she told me that my sister was alive and very sad. Unfortunately, her psychic ability didn't show her that my brother-in-law Gaspard was killed. Up to this day, no one knows what happened to him after he was taken from his house.

Even though my brother-in-law was a Hutu, his status didn't have any power or standing to people who were considered Hutu and called themselves Hutu Power. Since his mother was Tutsi, all the people in his family looked like Tutsis according to the classic definition used by Hutu extremists during the genocide. So, Gaspard's family didn't meet the requirements set by Hutu extremists. To the extremists, they were like the rest of us who were being hunted.

To be considered a Hutu at that time, you had to be short, unattractive, have a big nose, and have all the features that Belgians had set as the 'standard look of Hutus' during colonization. If you didn't have those characteristics or you had Tutsi blood in you, you were considers a Tutsi. Furthermore, my brother-in-law's father never agreed with the Hutu extremists on what they were doing, so for them, their family was considered enemies like the rest of us. Being a passive Hutu was considered a crime and it was almost a sin to the so-called 'real'

Hutus. Gaspard's family was doomed like the rest of us. Additionally, my brother-in-law had committed another crime by having a Tutsi wife.

Gaspard loved my sister so much. He was the most humble and wonderful man I had ever met. I can never forget him. I loved him and always hoped to have a husband like him when I grew up.

As I remained in the psychic's home she continued telling me that there is no way anyone would trespass her property and that it was protected. After two weeks, things changed. One day, Madame Zozo came home and told me that I couldn't live there anymore because she heard that murderers were going to come that night to kill me. She told me to go and sleep at her son's house, who was still single. And if for some reason they came, I could slip out and go into the bushes behind his house, and return after they left. Madame Zozo told me she would go the next day and get Tim to come and take me.

My journey was never over; there was no safe place in that country for me. I didn't understand how people continued to find out where I was every time I moved away. It seemed like death didn't want me, but neither did the earth. I wondered when all this running, hiding, and worrying would come to an end.

Chapter 11

"The Lord is my strength and my shield, my heart trusts in him and I am helped. My heart leaps for joy and I will give thanks to him in song."

~ Psalms 28:7

That night I slept at the psychic lady's son's house and waited for people to come and kill me, but no one came that night. The next day she went to tell my cousin's husband to come and take me away. That night, Tim came with his Twa friend Bubba. In those days, they were inseparable when it came to my rescue. We left that lady's house, but I thought - *now what?* I was always following people. I never knew where I was going to end up. At that time, both of them were scared as well; I didn't know if I would make it to another town. Then I found out that, after I had been with the psychic lady for a week, she had started going to my cousin's house every day asking for money from Tim to buy alcohol. It was then that people started to suspect that I was at her house because she was there so often. Otherwise, there would have been no way anyone would have found out where I was hiding.

Tim, Bubba, and I walked about an hour, and arrived at a place that seemed familiar. It was Bubba's house. Tim told me that from now on I was going to stay with Bubba's family until he figured out where to put me next, and that hopefully no one would suspect that I was there. I stayed there, but at this point I was numb and again questioning why I was alive. Every day I waited and wished to die, but death never passed my way.

Bubba had two wives who were living next to each other. It was common to find Twas with more than one wife. There are other people in Rwanda, non-Twas, who are not pygmies, who have more than one wife as well. But, it was not as common as in the Twas' society. Although polygamy was not legalized, it was not considered a real crime since no one got in trouble for it. Bubba continued to hide me in his home as a favor to Tim.

After living at Bubba's family's house for a week, he decided to build another house in an isolated place in the steep of the mountain where I could go hide. He said that, this place would be safer for me. It didn't take him a long time to finish construction. Bubba built a little house with two rooms and nothing else. In this new location, I moved in with his younger wife. Previously, I had been living with his older wife and her children.

What surprised me the most was how terrified his wives and children were of him. They respected him and didn't say anything the whole time I was there. For the entire genocide, I spent most of my time at Bubba's house. He told them that if they told anyone I was there, he would kill them. I was very surprised that even though they had very small children, not one word came out from them. Bubba told them to sit outside and watch for anybody suspicious who came near his house. And these little children did so. I remember this two-year-old who always used to come and peek at me and giggle. I didn't even respond to this little boy's giggle at that time as I had temporarily become mute, filled with sorrow. I just looked like a zombie; I don't even understand how this child was not afraid of me.

After we moved to the new isolated location, Bubba encouraged me to go outside to get some fresh air, but I refused for several days. Still, he kept insisting. He would go and sit outside in the evening, always assuring me that nothing would happen and he'd say that from where we were, no one could see me. Bubba would say if anyone ever comes down, he would cut them into pieces. I never wanted to go outside, I lived in constant fear.

The worst part was when I wanted to go to the bathroom in the middle of the day. The Twas never build bathrooms for inside their homes. Instead of having an actual bathroom, they built houses around bushes and then they would go to the bathroom in the bushes near their houses.

When I was living with his first wife; it was so hard for me to go outside when I needed to use the bathroom. First, I was terrified to go outside in the daylight; second, it seemed odd to go to the bathroom in an open place where anyone could see you. For some reason, even when I didn't eat that much, I still needed to go to the bathroom. I would ask one of children to make sure there was no one near their house so I could go.

So, when we moved into the new house with his second wife and there was no one in the house to look over me, I would urinate in the house when I couldn't hold it any longer. The foundation of the house was soft dirt so the urine got absorbed too quickly for anyone to discover. The problem came when I wanted to have a bowel movement; if no kids were around; I would dig a little hole in the corner of the room and then cover it up after I was finished. Bubba lived with one wife one week and the other wife the next. However, when we moved into the new house, he seemed to go over to his younger wife's house more often. I don't know if Bubba felt as though he had an obligation to stay there to protect me or if he was just enjoying his new home.

At some point, all those days that I was circulating from house to house, rumors were going around that I got killed in the other town two hours away from where my family used to live. I don't know who started the rumors; but luckily, people believed it for the time being, and they stopped searching for me. This tale allowed me to remain in Bubba's home for a long time..

After some time, I began feeling more relaxed and comfortable and so, in the evening, I would go outside to sit and watch the sunset. Often, I dreamt about the day I would be reunited with my whole family in heaven.

Then, one day when I was home alone, one of Bubba's sons, the one who wore my brother's sweater, tried to attack me. I was sitting inside of the house and it was about midday. I heard someone coming and was terrified, then when I looked up and saw that it was Bubba's oldest son, I was of kind glad. My thought was that at least I now had someone to talk to. Who was I kidding! No one cared about us. To most of the people, we were just targets for anything they wanted. Bubba came before his son succeeded with his evil mission; Bubba yelled at his son and told him if he ever touched me or got near me again, he would cut him into pieces.

This event just aggravated my awareness of hopelessness. There was no peace near me. If it was not people searching for me to kill me, there was insane people trying to jump on top of me. Aside from being a Tutsi, it was also a curse to be a woman during the genocide.

While I was at Bubba's house, Tim came to see me and told me that my auntie Felecite had been killed three weeks after I left his house. He told me that they marched her from the house to the middle of the town and killed her while everyone watched. She was killed along with a couple of children who were found in hiding nearby. A college-aged, beautiful young woman named Monique was also killed that day. She had been forced into a marriage during the genocide and had survived up until her husband felt he no longer needed her. I had been expecting that to happen. Nothing surprised me during that time. I just was envious of them for being killed: at least they were free from the fear and exhaustion that was plaguing me.

When Tim came to visit, he brought some old underwear with holes in it. I don't know where he got it from, but I guess it was his way of apologizing for what he had done. I was surprised that he remembered. After his failed attempt to rape me, I had been going around without underwear because he had cut mine to pieces. I took the dirty old underwear and wore it. The house we were staying in did not have proper plumbing and therefore, I hadn't' taken a bath since staying at my cousin's house, which had been a month now. To tell you the truth— taking a bath was the least of my concerns at that time. Who thinks about a shower when you are running for your life? After he left, I kept wondering when my time for death was going to come.

I stayed at Bubba's place for what seemed like forever. Around five or earlier in the morning before the sunrise, I would go and sit outside and wonder what was going to happen to me. Oh, how I dreamed of dying. Those moments of peace didn't last for long; I was not that lucky.

Chapter 12

"Why are you downcast, O my soul? Why so disturbed within me? Put your hope in God, for I will yet praise him, my Savior and my God."

~ Psalms 42:5

After that incident with Bubba's son, I thought about what Bubba had said and thought it was nice to have someone protect me, even temporarily. I would later learn that it was a ploy for what he had in store for me.

One day, Bubba came home drunk and decided that I had to repay him for all he had done for me thus far. This time no one was there, not even children who were almost always around. He had bloodshot eyes and if I knew what a devil looked like — he looked like one. For the first time, I was terrified of what was going to happen to me. My fate was ending. I was sitting on the bed. Bubba told me that I had to have sex with him, and there was no way out; I cried and pleaded with him not to do it. As I begged him to stop, he got so mad and told me that he was not wimpy like Tim and that I was not going to get away with being on the run this time. He grabbed me and threw me at the wall. He pulled my skirt up, and with a machete, cut my old underwear off. Déjà vu.

Bubba said if I fought him he would cut me to pieces. He went on telling me how Tutsi women were so ungrateful and that they would choose to die rather than have sex with a Hutus or a Twas. Did we think we were more special than anyone else? He told me how Hutus and Twas will start intermarriage because we were the ones holding everyone back from getting the husbands they wanted.

After this lecture, Bubba took his pants down with one of his hands and the other holding the machete. He got on top of me and tried to spread my legs. I kept fighting and hoping that he would give up like his friend and leave me alone, but he didn't. He slapped me across my face and hit me with the back of the machete. However, when I felt his nastiness touching my thighs, I thought I was going to die. I felt nauseous and couldn't breathe. I was shaking uncontrollably and was unable to remember much about what happened after that.

At some point, I dissociated my body from my mind, causing me to not be able to feel what was happening to me, or maybe that's how God protected me. Even when I tried very hard and dug deep to remember nothing comes, my memory seemed to go blank. After that, the only thing I remembered was Bubba lying next to my crumbled body, complaining that I didn't let him go inside of me. I remember getting up so quickly that I was crying, shaking, and throwing up, all at the same time. Then I could hear him on the bed praying to some kind of god to forgive him and hoping that he would conquer evilness and temptation.

I sat there under the bed for a long time — crying and was wondering why I wouldn't die like the rest of my family. Why was God allowing this happen to me? I felt so dirty and disgusting. And then I thought maybe that's what I was waiting on… so, I could die. For some reason, I thought maybe if I waited long enough under that bed, death might take me away. At some point, I think I fell asleep and when I woke up, the house was empty and no one was around. That day, I had a deep longing for death; but, against all odds, death rejected me.

My nightmare had become my reality. The fear of a rape that I had lived with for the entire genocide. After killings and other horrible things began happening, my thoughts of wanting to live began to fade. In fact, I didn't think I could live with what had just happened to me.

The curse I had for being born a Tutsi woman did not end with Bubba. Later, his sister in-law came to visit and she felt as though she could do whatever she wanted to me. We were like thrown away trash, any scavengers could go through, most of us Tutsi women, including myself, felt as though we were trash labeled with signs saying, "dig in", "rape", "kill", or "throw rocks". "All violations are welcome and encouraged."

We were sleeping in the same bed and Bubba's sister-in-law kept trying to put her fingers inside of me and I kept pushing them away. When she did not have her way, she kept rubbing herself on my leg until she had an orgasm. At that time, I did not know about or understand sexual behaviors. In my naiveté, I just thought she had peed on me, which, of course, made me think that she was a strange and quiet disgusting woman. Nevertheless, her behavior was very interesting and bizarre. I never knew a woman could do anything like this to another woman. I was young and naive, and had grown up sheltered in my village.

While all this happened to me, I remained quiet and could not even make a noise nor move. Who did I have to cry to? I was numb... even if I tried to scream out or tell someone what was happening to me, I would not have found any tears or been able to utter a sound.

I stayed with Bubba and his family for a while since I did not have anyone to cry to or any other place to go. After that incident, I had so much fear and hate toward him. I didn't want to be there anymore because every day I was reminded of how worthless I was. I never spoke a word to anyone there. On the contrary, I became mute and only answered when necessary. He would try to have little talks with me but I didn't respond. I just wanted to die so bad, I didn't see the point of continuing to live in this misery when in the end, I would be killed like the rest of my family.

Then, one day he came home and told me that people had found out I was still alive, and they were coming to kill me the next day. Why didn't he just let them come and kill me or kill me himself right then? I didn't understand how or why people would search for me so much – it was as if I were someone important.

In our neighborhood, people believed that our family had a lot of money even though we didn't. My family was believed to have been involved in the Rwandan Patriotic Front (RPF) because my brother Nkubili had been put in jail in 1990. And my other brother Mathias was believed to be an RPF soldier even though we didn't even know where he was either. So, to them, we knew and had a lot of secrets. What they didn't know was that my father was the least likely person to live a secretive life. He was an honest and open man.

Since he was the elected leader of our town, he was by de facto a member of the MRND (Mouvement Revolutionnaire National pour le Developpement) "National Revolutionary Movement for Development" party, which was the party of President Habyarimana. People would come from all over the towns around us to register to vote in our house. Come to think of it, if the RPF had gotten to our house earlier and seen how many voting cards were in our house, they might have thought we were the Interahamwe, the gang that French soldiers trained to kill like machines. Then we would have been in trouble with them as well.

I think my father had made peace with the fact that Hutus held the power, and there was nothing anyone else could do about it, besides doing the job he was assigned to in his town. So, I really didn't understand how a little person like me could be wanted so much. Our family was an open book. There was no secrecy, but during that time, people believed whatever they wanted to believe.

Chapter 13

"Be pleased, O Lord, to save me; O Lord, come quickly to help me. May all who seek to take my life be put to shame and confusion; may all who desire my ruin be turned back in disgrace. May those who say to me, "aha, aha!" be appalled at their own shame."

~ Psalms 40:13-15

Bubba told me that he had a hiding place for me. However, because of what had happened to me at the very hands of one of his family members, I was so afraid of him, and his family, nor did I trust him anymore. So, when he told me about the hiding place he had found for me, I wondered if it was not an excuse for getting me out of the house so he could kill me. Maybe it was an excuse to do what he wanted because Tim was not with him this time; and we hadn't heard or seen him in a while. However, since I had no other choice, I followed him. What did I have to lose anyway, a life I didn't have? We walked in the woods for a long time without talking. Sometimes he made small talk, but I don't think I responded. Finally, we got to this house hidden among banana plantations. When we got there, we met our hosts, an old man and his elderly wife. When I saw them, I was glad because usually older people in Rwanda, at least in the village where I grew up, were sincere and passionately protective toward young people. I thought, finally, maybe with this elderly couple, I could have a safe haven.

Bubba told me that no one would ever find me there. Then he left me. It had become normal for me to find myself in the homes of strangers.

Boy, was I wrong about these people. People who were living in Rwanda before the genocide were different from the ones I met during this horrible time. After a couple of days, I was in my new hiding location, and I observed that the old woman was strange and acting suspicious. Later, I found that her name was Mathilda and her husband's name was Yohani. Mathilda was not what I expected at all. Mathilda would look me up and down without saying a word, and I never understood why she looked at me like that. Before long, I began feeling uncomfortable. I started to ask myself why they even agreed for me to come and stay with them if they didn't want me there. Then again, probably Yohani is the one who talked to Bubba and told him that I could come and stay with them without Mathilda's consent. Mathilda seemed as if she didn't have much to say in her home. However, I didn't worry much about that because I had my own issues. In the end, this couple's business was not my concern.

Since, a banana plantation surrounded their home, no one could see their house. My new surroundings were a good situation for me. These people had a lot of land, which meant I was able to go outside for the first time in months without fear of being seen. I could do chores for Mathilda, with or without her, if there was someone nearby.

I lived there approximately one and a half weeks. After that, Yohani started being inappropriate; he would look at me in ways that made me uncomfortable. Yohani didn't say anything but his stare started to scare me. *What was wrong with these people?* His son, who lived in the house outside theirs, was the one who warned me about what his father was planning to do. He told me that whatever his father might ask me to do, I should decline. I couldn't believe Yohani was talking about making me his wife.

I knew in my fearful heart, I would rather die than become anyone's wife. What was wrong with these people? Was I carrying some kind of a sign on my forehead saying, "Rape me or make me your wife?" I couldn't understand. Then, after I heard this, I went and turned to his wife Mathilda thinking that she would support me. I told her that I preferred dying rather than being a wife at such a young age. She didn't say anything; Mathilda just gave me an evil look. Instead of supporting me, Mathilda brushed me off. Later, I found out that Mathilda's husband used to cheat on her with younger women. Yohani even brought them into their home. So, to her, I was a threat, not a victim, which is why she acted odd around me.

Back then in Rwanda, many men cheated on their wives and abused them, yet their wives stayed with them. This infidelity was mainly because women had no education or income to live on their own. Women felt there was no way to survive without their husbands and stayed with the cheating men despite all kinds of abuse. This was the reason this old woman had lived and dealt with all the disrespectful and abusive behaviors from her husband.

So later, Mathilda - instead of keeping confidential what we talked about, she went on and told her husband everything I had said to her. Her husband got so mad, probably because he was embarrassed about it. He decided to retaliate, although he didn't say anything to me. The next day Yohani went to tell Bubba that if he didn't come to get me, Yohani would throw me in the street and call my enemies to come and kill me.

During the genocide, a lot of men used the excuse of trying to help women by making them their wives, even though they killed them afterward; and that happened when they didn't want them anymore. What they didn't understand was that we women were already dead because we were having to live without our families and friends, whom they had already slaughtered.

Consequently, after Bubba heard what happened, he came with Tim and another friend. They told me that I had to go with them immediately, because if Yohani was to come home and find me in his house, that would be the end of my life. To tell you the truth, at this point, I was so exhausted, that the thought of dying was a welcome one. I was sick and tired of people abusing me, and I was tired of running from location to location in order to stay safely hidden. But since this was now happening in the middle of the day, and I was used to moving around in the dark, fear gripped me hard. I told them I was scared and asked why we couldn't wait until it got dark. Tim, Bubba and their new friend told me they would protect me.

That didn't change how I felt inside; but did I have any choice but to follow them?

The man who came with them I didn't know. Later, I learned that his name was Manzi and that he knew my family and went to school with my sister, Christina. He told me that my sister was very beautiful, smart, and nice but that he didn't know my family that well. Manzi told me that he heard that my parents were respectable people who loved and respected everyone. We all walked together for about thirty minutes; Manzi told Bubba and Tim that he would be happy to take me to his house. When Manzi said that he was going to take me, I thought to myself, here we go again, another nasty man. Bubba and Manzi agreed in unison. But, I told them I didn't want to go with Manzi. I wanted to go back with Tim. Tim said there is no way he would be able to get me to his house. It was farther and in the town. He said I would not survive that night if I went with him. Sadly, I didn't have any other options, and I couldn't go to either Bubba's or Tim's house. Manzi said bye to Bubba and Tim and told me to follow him. My journey never seemed to end.

On our way to his home Manzi saw that I was frightened and told me not to be afraid. I shook my head in agreement, but I was on guard because I didn't yet know or trust him. The guy was trying to make conversation all the way, but nodding or shaking my head was all he got in response. When we got to Manzi's house, I met his beautiful wife and two adorable children. He and his wife were a young couple and looked so happy together.

In my heart, I felt maybe things would be different here because I felt a good spirit in that house. Manzi's wife's name was Giselle and I learned she was very nice. When Giselle saw me, she was so sad and wanted to feed me. I knew this would be a better place, because no one had ever treated me this way the whole time I was in exile. Now, I can say that of all the places I stayed, including my cousin's house, this was the place that I felt most at peace. This couple was Seventh Day Adventist.

Chapter 14

"Forget the former things; do not dwell on the past. See, I am doing a new thing! Now it springs up; do you not perceive it? I am making a way in the desert and streams in the wasteland."

~ Isaiah 43:18-19

Every night Manzi and his wife Giselle prayed for me. I never heard anyone pray the way they prayed. They prayed to God as if He were someone they were talking with face-to-face and could tell anything in their heart. And I loved listening to these prayers. I grew up in a family where my father was a devoted Catholic who went to church every morning and never missed the Sunday services. But to me, it was just the routine of going to church. I never got the meaning of knowing God. Plus, my mother didn't go to church that much. She just went to church two times in a year, on Christmas, and on Easter. Once Mother mentioned that she used to go so much and then later, she had a lot of kids and stopped going to church. But now that I think about it, I trust that it was an excuse she gave for herself to feel better. I truly believe knowing my mom and how intimate and wonderful a person she was, the true reason was that after going to church for a long time and her not seeing a great deal of difference in her life, she felt it was meaningless to continue going.

Nevertheless, my father was very committed to Catholicism. I don't think he thought there was any true religion other than the Catholic Church. I remember one of my uncles sold his land to this Pentecostal pastor a little before the genocide started and built a church near our house. When it was completed, people came to pray and sing very loudly.

My father thought they were crazy, and since everyone respected him, sometimes he would go tell them to quiet down because they were making too much noise. Now, as I think about it, it's quite hilarious, someone going to a church and telling them to be quiet... and they obeyed my father's ridiculous order.

A little before the genocide started, I remember once they were shouting and praying in tongues and praising God so loudly. Since it was tense times for everyone, Dad marched to the church to tell them to go home. He thought they had nothing better to do than screaming.

Sometimes these born-again Christians would come to the church and stay for a week, fasting, and praying. When the fast was over, they had a party. They rejoiced, sang, and danced so loud. My father felt these Christians were spending too much time there and never saw the meaning of it. Dad thought they were lazy people who came there to escape from working. He was angry at my uncle for selling his land to these *crazy people*, as he called them.

I remember one of my teachers became a born-again Christian. He came to the church near my house, and then he came to visit and asked me to join them so he and other church members could pray for me and teach me. My father was there at that time, and he refused to let me go because of his distrust of them. He was distrustful, particularly of the fact that these Christians spent several evenings a week with young men and women praying together. "Who knows what else they might have been doing?" Dad said.

So, even though we used to pray together every night, my father led us in the prayers of Hail Mary and other Catholic prayers. Most of the time... as kids, we didn't take it seriously. While my father was praying, we were fooling around; pinching each other or slapping each other, in play of course. I remember my father would watch us fool around, never saying a word until he was done. However, by his look, we could tell that he couldn't wait to finish so we could get in trouble. My siblings and I didn't take the prayer time as seriously as he did, even though this was our nightly ritual.

I knew there was a God and knew that I could ask Him for help. But, I didn't feel a closeness or a strong relationship with Him. I didn't know the meaning and power of knowing God in my life, of knowing that I could tell Him anything I wanted as if I were talking to a friend. I didn't grasp the power of having God in my life and knowing Him personally until I began living with Manzi and his wife Giselle.

Living at their home was very enlightening for me in so many ways. Manzi and his wife truly prayed for me every night. And then Manzi gave me some verses from the Bible, which I will never forget. He taught me Psalm 23, which says *"The Lord is my shepherd, I shall not be in want. He makes me lie down in green pastures, he leads me beside quiet waters, he restores my soul. He guides me in paths of righteousness for his name's sake. Even though I walk through the valley of the shadow of death, I will fear no evil, for you are with me; your rod and your staff, they comfort me. You prepare a table before me in the presence of my enemies. You anoint my head with oil; my cup overflows. Surely goodness and love will follow me all the days of my life, and I will dwell in the house of the Lord forever."* After he read this psalm for the first time, I felt as if it were God Himself who was reading the words to me. A sense of peace and joy overcame me - flooding my heart like never before. I believe something changed in me that day. This Psalm helped me to know that God protected me no matter what was going on around me. This also helped me to realize that if my time had not yet come, I was still protected by God. And if I died, it would not be just up to the Hutus who were continuously hunting me but according to God's plan. Manzi and Giselle also taught me songs that helped me through that time. I started to pray and read the Bible they had given me.

For the first time, since the beginning of this horrendous experience, I really do not know what came over me, but now, I wanted to live. I promised God that if He saved my life, I would never hate anyone again. I would forgive those people who had killed my family and had taken my innocence away. From that time onward, I had a peace in my heart and deep down, I knew I was not going to die, even though I couldn't see how I was going to live. I kept wondering where I was going to live. Even though, I was willing to forgive the Hutus who assassinated my family, I didn't think I could live with them the way we had lived before.

Most likely, the promises I made with God at that moment helped me to get through the Genocide. I really was not bitter, although, I was very sad and depressed because I had lost most of my family. However, the good thing was I didn't have hatred in my heart. And today, I thank God for that covenant we made together in that dark room at Manzi's house because it helped me to recover from the trauma.

I stayed with Manzi and Giselle for a long time. They lived in an isolated place in the valley of the hill. There was no neighbor in near sight. The location they lived in was pretty much isolated; except the empty burned-out homes that belonged to Tutsis who used to live in the area before they got killed or escaped and flew far away from their houses. Therefore, when I was there, the fear of someone seeing me or coming there vanished. For the first time in a long time, I felt safe when I was staying with them.

And no one ever came to their house.

However, Manzi lived next door to his parents. At his parents' house were a lot of people. Some were his relatives who had migrated from the Eastern side of Rwanda (Kibungo) during Genocide when RPF and Rwandan armies were fighting. Among the people who were staying with his parents, was Manzi's nephew who was in his early twenties. Manzi's nephew was a very angry young man and hated RPF soldiers. Their house was packed with refugees.

At the end of June, his nephew began to get scared. Manzi told me that the RPF soldiers were getting close. He told me that his whole family needed to leave soon because when the RPF got there, he and his family would be killed. That was news to me. First, I was being hunted by Hutus, and now Hutus were scared that Tutsi soldiers were going to kill them. Manzi's nephew had this big stick he had carved and rounded on the top. Afterward, nails were put on the top part. Then Manzi's nephew told me that before he left, he would kill me with it because he was not going to let me live and be rescued by the RPF soldiers. Instead of being happy that the RPF soldiers were approaching, I began to wish that they would stay away so I would not be killed. The first few times Manzi's nephew told me this, I just ignored him. However, when he repeated the warnings to me over and over again, I realized that he was serious. I told Manzi what his nephew was planning to do. Manzi told me not to worry because he was never going to let him do anything to me. He said that his nephew was just bitter because he had been forced out from his home and he was terrified. Manzi called him selfish because he didn't look beyond his situation to see the suffering of others.

Then at the beginning of July, Tim, and Bubba came to Manzi's house in the middle of the day. At that point, I had forgotten about Tim. I wanted to forget about him because I knew that every time Tim showed up, there was something happening, spreading bad news or I feared he was coming to take me away again. When I saw Tim, I wondered where I was going to next. As I suspected, Tim told me that I had to leave right away. But when he saw how scared I was, Tim told me not to worry that there was no one looking for me. Tim said that maybe this would be my lucky day, but he didn't tell me anything else.

They put me in a long heavy jacket, a hat and rushing me out of the house. Bubba, Tim, had machetes when they come to see us. Then Manzi grabbed a machete as well and came with us, but I didn't know

85

where they were taking me. They ordered me to walk between them. Manzi, Bubba, and Tim saw the fear in my eyes and assured me that someone in order to get to me, they must go through them. In my mind, I was thinking where are they taking me now in the middle of the day, while people could be watching.

I thought, after all being at Manzi's had been too good to be true. Still, there was no way it was going to last forever. Since, I didn't have a choice, as always, I followed them. On the way, Tim explained that he had been conversing with the French soldiers who were camping near where my family used to live. For a week Tim went to the French soldier's camp and begged them to take me into a safe location. In the beginning, they refused and told him 'no'. However, every day he would wake up and go there again and plead with them. I think at some point they got tired of seeing him and finally told him to go and bring me the next day. By this time, in July, the RPF had captured most of some parts of Rwanda, except for the place we were located. Thus, there were parts of Rwanda that was safe and there were places where they were not people still killing Tutsi in a broad daylight. However, at Munini, Gikongoro, where I am from, the killings were still occurring. That's the reason Tim was trying so hard to get me out of there because French soldiers had a way to move me to a location was safe.

First, they refused but, that very morning before Tim and Bubba came to Manzi's house, the French soldier had told Tim to bring me. They had finally agreed to take me to a safe location. Tim, Manzi, and Bubba and I walked probably for two hours to get to the French soldiers' camp location. It took us longer because we didn't go on the regular road. We walked through woods and burned houses where a lot of Tutsis used to live before the genocide.

As Tim, Manzi, Bubba, and I were walking, I didn't trust I would survive; I suspected my life could be coming to an end. My guardians were a little scared, too; you could hear their heavy breathing even if they were trying to cheer me up, and they were extremely anxious to get me to the French soldiers' safely. Now that I think about it, even though these men committed cruel, gruesome acts, God used them to save my life.

On the way there, we met a young guy named Nzovu, who went to school with my older brother Damascene. Nzovu was so surprised to see me alive. He looked like he had seen a ghost. "Is that Anamaliya? This can't be true that she is still alive," he mumbled to himself. Nzovu asked the men where they were taking me. They didn't respond to him. Tim, Manzi, Bubba, and I just kept walking fast and sometimes even running. Nzovu stopped from where he was going and turned around and followed us. At that moment, I was so scared. I knew if this guy gave the word my life would be over. That's what usually happened when someone saw a Tutsi. But, to my surprise, and by the grace of God, Nzovu didn't say a word. He just kept running after us.

Finally, we reached the soldiers at their camp. To get there, we had passed my house. I looked at it and wondered if my reality that day had all been a nightmare. My prayer would be to wake up and discover everything had been a bad dream. When we got to the French soldiers' camp, they were almost ready to leave. Tim talked to them for what seemed like a lifetime. Around us people were staring, I was thinking if somehow something goes wrong, I will be meat to these beasts. I was standing between Manzi and Bubba with their machetes alert as if they were ready to attack. Then finally, Tim came back and told me to get into a jeep that was already running. Tim, Bubba and Manzi said goodbye. Tim, who must have thought those soldiers were taking me to France or to God knows where, told me not to forget them. I nodded my head in agreement with him because he was so happy that I had survived. Tim looked very satisfied and so relieved. I guess to Tim, he felt so happy and that there had been a big accomplishment that at least Tim had successfully saved one person from his wife's family.

I said bye to my guardians and started another journey. Still, it confused me as why they looked so happy.

Chapter 15

"Can a mother forget the baby at her breast
and have no compassion on the child she has
borne? Though she may forget I will not forget
you! See, I have engraved you in the palms of my
hands; your walls are ever before me."

~ *Isaiah 49:15-16*

At this time, I really did not care about much anymore. This, to me, was another phase of this three-month long struggle. It was different people, a different place, and this time, it happened to be white people I couldn't even understand. I nodded my head and got inside the jeep.

The young guy who had been following us was so angry. He shouted something about the fact that I was lucky to have survived. I had no idea what he was talking about. What did he mean *survive*? I didn't understand what he was talking about. In that jeep was a couple, their children, and an older woman whom I guessed was the man's mother. I think the woman was a Tutsi and her husband was a Hutu.

Quite naturally, they were having a hard time in the area where they lived, because they wanted to kill his wife. The couple asked if they could leave that place and luckily, the French soldiers let them leave. There were three jeeps traveling together. We were in the middle vehicle. The ones in the front and back of us carried soldiers with guns.

All the jeeps were open in the back, which made me feel unsafe. Besides, I really didn't trust these French people. First of all, from what I heard, they didn't really want to take me. Secondly, their county supplied machetes and trained youth Hutu gangs who were responsible for massacring my people. To top it off, they were there during half of the genocide, but they didn't do much. To me, it was just the routine of my life, going from one place to another. That's how I looked at it, as if God had not given up on me yet.

While traveling in those jeeps, we passed by one of my neighbor's kids. We used to hang out together. He looked at me with such anger, and I couldn't understand why. I should have been the one who looked at him like that since his family and his relatives had killed my family and had destroyed my life. Then I met more… along the way, someone yelled, "You are lucky you didn't get killed."

People everywhere were yelling and screaming, "I see Tutsis in that car," or "are those Tutsis in those white people's car?" "Is that Anamaliya? I can't believe she is still alive!" like as if it was a sin for us to be alive. We continued driving and it seemed like a never-ending ride.

Later in the afternoon, we arrived at a place with a lot of people. Some were laughing; I couldn't believe there were people who were still laughing. *What was going on here? Was this the same country I had been living and hiding in for the last three and a half months, horrified for my life every day?* Those were the questions going on in my head. When we got there, the soldier ordered us to get out of the car. They handed me to a guy who was probably in his middle or late twenties.

When the man saw the tension and the fear in my eyes, he pleaded with me not to be frightened. "I am like you, and I will not harm you," he promised. What did he mean he was like me? Was there any Tutsis like him still alive and talking as though nothing happened? I couldn't believe it. *Was this real?* Or, was I still dreaming? *Did I really survive? Was my life no longer in danger?* The man gave me a box of cookies and a blanket, then sent me to the house full of kids right there in the camp. These kids were all orphans who survived the genocide. In the camp, all the children slept on the floor. I really don't remember much about the inside area of the house where the orphans were; the only thing I remember is how many children there were. Many of them had wounds on their heads, arms, legs, and other parts of their bodies. These children were so young and didn't know where they were from or their parents' names. Some of them didn't remember their own names.

Looking at them, I didn't feel sorry for myself any longer. I saw people more injured and vulnerable than I was. At least I still had both of my legs and arms. I didn't get hurt physically, only emotionally and deep in my heart where no one could see or touch.

After a couple of days of living in the camp, I saw children who had been neighbors to my sister. I was so happy to see them. I asked them if my sister and her husband were still alive. They said they all had been killed. Again, I lost hope and was overcome by a deep depression. I couldn't imagine living in the world without even one of my siblings. *Where was I going to go?*

After spending time with the children in the orphanage I decided that maybe I could stay with them to help and to comfort them. Actually, a couple of the kids grew very attached to me while I was there. Because I was still shaken by my cousin's daughter Clarisse's death, I didn't want to get too attached to the needy children. However, I loved being near them even though they made me no feel so alone – as my heart was aching for my own family.

The place we were staying at was a camp that was occupied and protected by French soldiers. This was the part of Rwanda where the French soldiers were operating. The location was called "Zone Turquoise", or "Operation Turquoise" was the name of the French military operation in Rwanda.

After a week of living in the orphanage, I saw people from my village who lived in Kigali, but who fled there during genocide and had ended up at Gikongoro. There were two women and a guy named Andre. One of these women was Andre's sister-in-law named Olive. Olive had a little baby. The second woman's name was Salapie and she was Olive's friend. Salapie was pregnant. Andre's family lived near where we had lived. I was so happy to see someone from our old neighborhood – people who were still alive. Andre, Olive, and Salapie invited me to come and live with them instead of living in the orphanage. I was glad to go live with Andre and his family because living with wounded children like me truly causing me more depression.

Olive, Andre, and Salapie were also living with a young woman from my town named Claudette. Claudette was Olive's live-in-nanny, before genocide. Claudette and Olive had fled together when the genocide began. They escaped from Kigali together. Olive and Salapie neither knew if their husbands were alive or dead. I liked both Olive and Salapie, but I really liked Salapie, the pregnant one the best. I lived with them for a while and waited for things to settle. Salapie told me that since neither of us had family left, when things were safe for us to go back to Kigali that she would be glad to bring me to live with her.

We lived there for a while and then UNAMIR (The United Nations peacekeeping force) trucks began to take people who wanted to go to the zone where the RPF had taken over. At that time, the RPF had taken over all the parts of the country except southern Rwanda. People who committed genocide were packed into these areas. That's why the place where we were staying was secured by French soldiers.

In southern Rwanda, the genocide was still prevalent. Genocidaires knew that their time was coming to an end but they had not given up yet. They were still killing people in this little area and they were also still holding on to their way. There were people at the Zone Turquoise who had committed genocidal acts and were living in that camp pretending to be survivors.

What the UNAMIR did was trade people. They would bring people who wanted to leave the RPF occupied place and go into Zone

Turquoise where the French soldiers were supposedly keeping peace. Then in return, UNAMIR packed people from Zone Turquoise who wanted to go to the RPF zone. So, people who wanted to go to the RPF areas were driven by the UNAMIR trucks from Gikongoro to Butare. Salapie, Andre, Olive, and her nanny Claudette decided what day we were going to leave that place. The UNAMIR trucks took us the next morning and dropped us at the border of Gikongoro and Butare in a town called Maraba. We found a vacant house, went in, and lived in it. I don't remember much about the place, but I remember the house was surrounded by an abundance of banana trees, there were cloths everywhere and food on the stove. It looked like the people who lived in the house rushed to get out and didn't take much with them. I think the house belonged to the Hutus who fled away from the RPF soldiers when they got there. We 'stayed' there about a week until we found a ride to Butare city.

When we got to Butare, Salapie and her friend Olive met a man they knew from Kigali. He took us to his house, which was close to where my sister used to live. The first thing I did when I got there was to go to my sister's house to confirm that no one was there. When I arrived, I discovered the house was destroyed, and the roof of the house contained holes; there were no windows or doors. There was nothing in the house except pictures and paper scattered all over the place. After I saw what the place looked like, I knew that everyone was gone. I kept thinking if the Hutus murders did this to my sister's house, then there was no telling what they did to the owner of the house.

I proceeded to pick up the pictures, which were laying all over the place, and then I left. Now, realizing so much, I went back where I was staying knowing that no matter what, if God left me alive, maybe He had a plan for me.

At this point, none of us had clothes except for what we were wearing. However, when we got to Butare, people found things in the homes of families who had fled during the fighting. Actually, people were getting greedy about it, and went around raiding the abandoned homes. Personally, I didn't care. I never went to get any of the belongings left behind. I could care less. I knew my family has several possessions. Where were they now? Material things didn't interest me at all. Olive's nanny Claudette went crazy going around inside the people's houses taking things. All I cared about was that I could finally take a shower for the first time in three months... without being scared and wondering when I was going to be killed or when someone might jump on top of me. My energy was spent mourning for my family. Claudette felt sorry for me and brought me back some clothes. Their friend also brought me clothes. Olive and Salapie's friend, the man we were staying with randomly brought me things.

I thought it was nice of him until I found out that he planned to convince these women to leave me behind when they left for Kigali so he could make me his wife. The nanny made fun of me and thought it was funny but I found it disgusting. This man, who should have considered himself my brother and my protector wanted to do the same thing to me as the other men I had encountered. I started thinking something was wrong with me. Salapie however got scared because the guy was an RPF soldier she didn't know what he was capable of doing. She told me not to worry and that she was not going to tell him when we were leaving. Salapie continued to try and find a ride that would get us back to Kigali.

Meanwhile, when we were staying in Butare waiting for transportation, one day, Salapie and I went to the city; I met one of my cousins Vincent who lived in Kigali before the genocide. Vincent was Clarisse's uncle - the little girl I was holding before the killing of my own family. I was so happy to see him. I couldn't believe one of my relatives was still alive. My cousin Vincent was married, and he was going to Burundi to find his wife because they got separated during the genocide. The first time he saw me though, he didn't recognize me at all. He was so traumatized, I felt sorry for him. Vincent said to me, "I think I know you." I told him my name, thinking he would realize who I was. He asked, "Who is your father?" Oh, my God! I couldn't believe someone who knew me all my life would forget me in three and half months. I told him more about who I was. Vincent asked me if anyone had survived in our town. I told him nobody except me. He started to cry, and literally began sobbing.

At this time, I don't think I had any feelings, I was like a rock, tears did not come easily to me. This was a man who was in his late thirties to early forties and I felt sad for him. I was thankful that I wasn't like him and I still had a clear mind. My cousin Vincent told me that he was going to get his wife from Burundi because she fled there after her brothers had killed her son. Vincent's wife was a Hutu, so during the genocide she had told her husband since she couldn't take him with her; she was going to her parents to save her son. However, when she got to her parents' house, her brothers told her they couldn't let her son live because it was unheard to have a Tutsi boy. So, her brother took her son and killed him. At this time, she was pregnant as well and her brother told her that if she give birth to a son, he'll be killed too.

After they killed her son, she fled to Burundi to save her unborn child. When I met my cousin Vincent in Butare, his behavior seemed crazy. Vincent couldn't believe that his brother-in-law could kill his own son. We talked for a while and then he gave me five thousand Francs and told me to buy what I needed. He said that when he got back from Burundi, he would pass by and take me to go live with him. I was so happy that at least one of my relatives was still alive, even though he did not seem to be the cousin I once knew and respected. I didn't care about the money that he gave me. I handed it over to Salapie.

PART III: Aftermath
Chapter 16

"Call to me and I will answer you and tell you great and unsearchable things you do not know."

~ Jeremiah 33:3

We were in Butare for a couple of weeks, and I hadn't heard back from my cousin Vincent. I decided to go with Salapie. When we got to Kigali, I was going to look for my cousin. However, before we left, a man who used to be a teacher at my elementary school came to visit us. The teacher told me that my sister Christina was still alive, and that she was living nearby. At first, I didn't believe him. Because he knew my family well, I thought that he could be right. But on the other hand, compared to how my own cousin couldn't even recognize me, anything was possible with these people who survived genocide. This teacher also told me that my sister's daughter Gabby was also alive, and he had seen my sister Christina at the hospital where she worked nearby. He informed me where Christina was staying, what time she went to work, and where she passed by. When the teacher said about her working at the hospital, I slightly believed him; my sister was a nurse I thought maybe he might be right and it would not hurt to go and check out things.

At this time, Butare was desolate. So many damaged homes, corps still lying on ground, the air smelled of death and rotting flesh, and so much brokenness everywhere you turned. There were so many people but everyone looked somber. There were still dark clouds hovering over our country of Rwanda. People were confused and in disbelief of the nightmare we had just survived. It was chaos; people didn't know whether to start picking up the pieces or sit and mourn. Survivors joined together and lived in houses because no one wanted to live alone. People invited people from the street into their homes. It was hard to know if any of your loved ones survived because people moved and went to live with other people. There was unity and love among the survivors.

Since I didn't know exactly where she lived, I decided to get up early to go sit where the teacher told me Christina passed by every morning. The first day I woke up at five-thirty and sat there until nine. I didn't see her, so I went back home and decided to get up earlier the next day. Nevertheless, I didn't see her then either. I repeated this routine for a week. Then I gave up.

However, more people kept telling me Christina was alive, but I didn't believe them anymore, because I didn't want to be disappointed any more than I already was. Consequently, I returned to my loneliness and gave up the thought that someone in my family might be alive. Two days before I was going to Kigali, Salapie rushed home to tell me that she had spoken with my sister. Since it was late, Salapie told me that the next day we would go together to see Christina. That night I was so excited I couldn't wait for the following morning. If it was up to me, I would have walked there in the night to see her. The night seemed so long. My excitement kept me from being able to sleep. The next morning, I got up and waited anxiously for Salapie to get ready. I was fidgeting and I couldn't sit still. I spent much of the morning walking in circles around the living room. Finally, she got up and took me to see my sister.

On our way there I couldn't contain myself—inside I wanted to burst with happiness. When I finally saw my sister, I was so joyful for the first time in months I broke down and sobbed uncontrollably. I couldn't believe she was still alive. My own sister Christina, it was a miracle! I also saw my nieces Gabriella and Carine, my older brother Nkubili's daughter. They all were so skinny and poignant. It was heartbreaking to see them compared to what they looked like before the genocide. Still, I was thrilled to be able to find some family members and couldn't hold my happiness. All this time, I had searched for her in the wrong location. The place I had sat for those early mornings was the wrong location which is why I had never seen her.

Christina told me that people had been telling her that one of her little sisters was still alive, but she didn't believe them for a while either. She had been wondering how in the world I could have ended up where I was. It was unreal. She was afraid to come to see if I really was alive. Christina didn't want to be disappointed either, but that very same day I went to see her, my sister said she had also determined to come and look for me for her own peace of mind. In the days and months after the genocide, many survivors were on the search for relatives who had also survived. People traveled miles and miles to find their loved ones because of the rumors they heard and in the end found nothing. It was a very had time for survivors. This was one of the reasons my sister didn't bother coming to search for me when people told her they had seen me.

I asked Christina how she got Carine since I knew she was living in Kigali with her parents. Her answer was that throughout the genocide, Carine was with her because a neighbor friend of Carine's family knew that her parents were going to be killed. The neighbor took Carine when he fled Kigali and brought her to a friend of Christina's. Then Christina went to get Carine because at that time the genocide had not reached Butare yet.

This time with family was a celebration for me. I couldn't believe that some of my family members had survived. I thanked God, and I am still thanking Him today. Not just because He kept His promise of me not getting killed, but also because He gave me more than I was expecting. I was not only a survivor, but God had also protected the lives of my loved ones and reunited us.

At that time, my sister was living in a large home with other survivors. Everyone cooked and ate together. As we spent many days and evenings together, it became a tight-knit community. There was warmth, love, and even laughter, as we began to start rebuilding the routines of 'normal lives' after months of horror. I think this was the way we coped with what happened to all of us. We lived there for a couple of months. My sister Christina looked depressed every day. It was not easy for her; she was staying in the same location she had lived in before genocide. Being there every day was a reminder of the pain of losing her husband, and all the people she loved who had been slaughtered. I didn't think I would have been able to live in the same place I had lived in before the genocide either. It was heartbreaking for her. Christina told me that she needed a change and needed to move away. My sister told me that she had friends in Kigali who survived the genocide and that my sister wanted to go and visit them. She wanted to see if she could also find a job in Kigali. Christina told me when she got a job and a house that she would come and take me with her. So, after a couple of months of living with her in Butare, my sister decided to move to Kigali. Christina took the girls with her since they were little and left me with the people we were living with. Those people were nice so it was like a family.

While we were still living in Butare, we found out that two of our brothers Mathias and Jean Damascene were alive. Mathias had joined the RPF after 1990. All those years we never knew he was alive. My other brother Damascene was in Rwanda during the genocide. He was very fortunate that RPF took over where he was hiding and he had joined the military during the genocide. So, compared to many survivors who were left without any of their loved ones, we felt fortunate.

A couple of weeks after my sister moved to Kigali, she came back to Butare. When Christina came back, she said one of our second aunts was alive and was living with her son in Kigali. My aunt told Christina to move in with her instead of living with her friend. Our aunt insisted that she come to get me as well. So, my sister Christina and I moved to Kigali and lived with our aunt. When we were living with her, our aunt was still searching for her four other children. Eventually, she found her girls, and youngest son. Her children all came back from Congo and we all lived together in her three bedroom house. After a short while, my sister found an apartment and she and I and my nieces moved in it.

I wasn't in school at that time; instead, I stayed home and cooked, cleaned, and did laundry for all of us while my sister worked at Roi Faycal, a hospital in Kigali. When she got paid, Christina handed me the money because I was the one who shopped for the house. However, as days went by, my sister became stressed. She was constantly working and then going back and forth from Butare to Kigali to rebuild her house that was destroyed during genocide. These were not easy times for her. As for me, I was having the time of my life with my nieces and was so glad that I had my family around me. Christina, however, was getting worse emotionally and physically. She was physically exhausted from working nonstop at the hospital because they were short on staff and the small amount of time off she got, she used it to travel to Butare and Kigali back and forth to work on her home. Christina barely had any rest. And emotionally she had lost many of her close friends, husband, and family. She was the only adult in our household and we all depended on her. All this had so much weighed on her emotionally. One of her sisters-in-law advised her to get out of the country and move away from it all. They invited her to come and live in Kenya with them.

My sister wanted to go to Kenya, but she didn't know how she would be able to take us all. So, Christina sat me down and assured me that she was not abandoning me. She told me that she had to relocate, but, would return for me as soon she settled down. Of course, I was sad, still, I knew there was no other choice. Besides, my sister now had three children, on her shoulders who were all under six-years of age. I was old enough to be able to stay there for a while. Before she left, Christina went and asked our aunt, the one we used to live with, if she would keep me for a while. My aunt said *no* because there were already a lot of people in her house and there was no place for me. I was so disappointed and sad when my sister told me my aunt's decision. I had no other relatives and no other place to go. It hit me for the first time after the genocide that I really was an orphan, and even worse, an unwanted one. My sister was really worried because she didn't have a place to leave me.

Fortunately, while Christina was trying to find a place for me, she met one of our distance cousins Nadine and explained our situation to her. Thank goodness, my cousin happily agreed to house me. Needless to say, Christina was so relieved.

My cousin Nadine was young—probably in her mid-twenties. When she was going to college before the genocide, she lived at my brother Nkubili's house, and every time Nadine took a vacation, she came to visit us. I knew her well and was happy to go live with her; I saw her as my older sister, as well. Shortly after that, my sister left me in the apartment we were living at. Before Christina left, she tried to work on getting a passport for me. At that time, getting a passport was difficult but she managed to get me a laisser passé. With this laisser passé, you could travel to neighboring countries around Rwanda.

Christina, Carine, Aurore, and Gabriella left. The day they moved I cried and wondered when I was going to see them again. I felt so alone once again; it was a reminder that my parents no longer exist on this earth. At the end of the month, I packed my belongings and went to live with my cousin.

When I got to Nadine's house, I discovered that she was living with her older sister, and her cousin Dative. The house they stayed in

100

had two bedrooms, a small kitchen, and a living room. Nadine had one of the big rooms with king-sized bed, while her older sister had a simple bed in her little room. In the kitchen, there was a bed with a little mattress like the one you put in a crib. I thought maybe that's where they sat when they were cooking.

Later, I found out that Dative, their cousin, was sleeping on that little mattress in the kitchen. When it was time to go to bed, I thought maybe I was going to have to sleep in the same room with Nadine or her older sister. Nadine told me that I had to go and sleep with Dative in the little kitchen room. At first, I thought she was joking, because I didn't even think Dative could fit on the mattress… let alone, the two of us trying to fit in the small dirty kitchen.

Dative was maybe in her mid-thirties. Nadine looked down on her because she didn't know how to read or write. To them, it was a favor to keep Dative in their house. I couldn't believe that someone would treat his or her family member like that. Nadine turned out to be someone I really didn't recognize anymore. She was not the girl I used to know and admire – the one who used to visit us before the genocide. Dative and I slept on that little mattress and no one breathed or moved because if we did either one of us, we could have ended up on the floor. Nadine always commented on how my brother and his wife were so good to her. However, at some points, I wanted to ask her if for some reason she had been treated badly at my brother's and I was now paying the price for something I didn't even know about. It was difficult to believe someone so young could be so cruel.

While staying there, I cooked and cleaned the house, which I really didn't mind, since I was home and my gratitude needed to be known.

All my efforts to help were never appreciated. Since we didn't have any water inside the house, if in the morning Nadine didn't find a bucket of water to take a bath, she would yell. Even though, the water was two-steps away between our house and our landlord's. She was a very difficult person to live with, almost all the time. However, if you saw her outside you would never know she was that kind of person. What kept me going was the hope that I probably wasn't going to live there for a long time. I had to keep reminding myself that my sister would come back for me soon and that situation was temporary. At that point, I had been through a lot worse than living with a difficult woman.

Before my sister Christina left, she told me periodically to go over to one of her friend's Julienne's house for an update on her and the girls. Also, she left money with Julienne in case I needed anything. Julienne also was the one who was responsible for picking up Christina's pay, because she was still officially on paid vacation. So, because of this I had to go to see Julienne from time to time. Nadine was unhappy with everything. She thought I was looking for an excuse to leave the house, even though I made sure that before I left, the house was cleaned and the food was cooked.

A few months after my sister left, I got sick with malaria. I thought I'd die if I stayed at Nadine's place. I was in bed sick for a week and no one even asked me how I was doing or offered to take me to the doctor or even buy me some medication. I dragged myself from the bed, took a taxi and went to Julienne's house. Luckily, I could go stay with Julienne and her husband. I stayed there with them for a short time, because Julienne was a nurse and could help me get well. Through all this, Nadine didn't feel any sympathy, empathy, or pity for me. She kept saying that she suspected that I was faking my illness. I never asked her for anything… not even for fifty cents to take a cab. When finally, I couldn't take it anymore, I explained my situation to Julienne and her husband. Since they had a lot of people living with them, Julienne and her husband really didn't have a space for me to stay for a long time.

My brother Damascene was with me when I went to talk with Julienne and her husband. Damascene was visiting because he had a day off from the army. We sat with Julienne, and her husband to try to figure out what to do. Then the husband had an idea. He told me that they had a friend and Christina knew this family as well, who needed a

102

nanny. Julienne's husband suggested that I go and live there and work for them as a nanny and that no one would know. He said that they would treat me good, and besides, he added, "Christina has three little children, there is no way she will come back for you, but if you take this job, you will have the money and a place to stay at the same time." I couldn't believe my ears. I didn't have a place to go and my options were going to be the nanny of the friend of my sister's. I knew my friend had said this out of love and didn't want to seem unhappy.

The job of being a nanny in Rwanda is not like the same job as it would be here in America. A nanny job at this time, was the lowest paying job that one could have. People treated them like second-class citizens, which is very unfortunate, but that's the way it was then. When Julienne's husband told me this, I was so hurt I wanted to burst out crying, but I held back my tears.

My brother Damascene sat there and didn't say one word. I told them that I would think about it, but in my mind, there was nothing to think about at the time. I had enough baggage on my life I didn't have to add to even more to it. Even though Nadine was treating me like a house girl in her home at least she was so-called family. After this conversation, Damascene walked with me to get a cab, the whole way I kept sobbing, all the tears I had held come down so hard, all the way tears were dripping on my face. Damascene didn't even know how to console me, I was hysterical. I couldn't believe what was happening to me. One minute I had a family and was so happy and the next minute, no one who seemed to want me. It became like during the genocide all over again, except this time, my life was no longer at risk. Everyone seemed to believe that my sister would never come back for me. This claim was just something I really didn't want to believe. I hoped my sister would prove them wrong. However, over time, I became discouraged. *"What if's"* occupied my mind daily. *What if she doesn't come back for me, what would happen to me?*

In Kenya, Christina was living with her sister-in-law and three little girls with no job. I thought about taking the nanny job but my pride just wouldn't let me do it, especially not working for someone who knew my sister. As desperate as I was, I couldn't do it. As I began weighing my options, I found out that I miraculously had passed the national exam. In Rwanda, before you go to high school you must take the national exams. Most high schools required you to go to a boarding school. When I discovered that I had passed the exam to go to high school, I was so happy. At least I had a place to go for a couple of months. I thought that I would deal with where I would stay during the break when I crossed that bridge.

School was due to begin in four months, but this just wasn't coming quickly enough for me—it was four months away. After you pass the exam, the Minister of Education assigns you to whatever school they want. I was sent to a high school near where we used to live. When I found out where I was assigned, I was so scared because I had to go through my hometown to get there. I didn't want to go back there. I didn't feel emotionally ready to return to my hometown. I felt that I was not ready to even see home again, never mind going to live there.

While I was struggling to decide what to do about the school, Christina called to see how I was doing. Julienne told her the news about my exam results and told my sister where I was sent. My sister insisted that I shouldn't go to the high school in my hometown. She instructed me to go look for one of her nun friends who was a headmistress at a high school in Gitarama, to see if she could transfer me to her school. The headmistress agreed to transfer me, but she said I had to attend the school I was assigned to first. Then, after a year, I could get my transfer. Since I had no other better choice, I took that one.

While I was waiting for school to start, I was still at Nadine's house. I couldn't wait to leave. I had three long months remaining before I could leave. Luckily, while I was still there, one of my cousins Noreen, who migrated from Uganda, came looking for me. Noreen asked around and found where I lived and visited me at Nadine. I had met Noreen before but only briefly before my sister was just about to go to Kenya. I never thought about her until she came back to find me. Noreen and her family grew up in Uganda, she never knew us and we had not known them.

Noreen's parents fled to Uganda during the killing of 1959. Noreen was born and raised in Uganda with her siblings. She and her sister moved to Rwanda after the RPF took over. When Noreen and her family arrived in Rwanda, they searched for our oldest brother Nkubili—the one who had died during genocide. He was the only one Noreen and her family knew, no one else. Nkubili was the only one who used to sneak in to go visit them in Uganda. However, people told them Nkubili had been killed, but that his sister Christina was still alive. Noreen came looking for her and that was the time that Christina was in the process of leaving the country. Christina didn't tell her anything about her travel plans. When Noreen went back to visit at the place my sister and I used to live, she didn't find anybody there. However, our landlord told her that Christina had gone to Kenya. They provided Noreen the address of where I was staying and then Noreen came to look for me at Nadine's house.

After that first time Noreen came to visit me, she saw how I was living. Seeing things were not good, she invited me to live with her. I hesitated, since I didn't know her that well and because of all the disappointments I had experienced. I didn't want to get hurt, yet again. I promised Noreen that I would go and at least visit. She was so sweet natured and always smiling. After she left, I kept thinking about her offer.

A couple of weeks went by and I decided to go visit Noreen, I went and spent the weekend with Noreen and her younger sister Vicky. They were so nice to me that I really didn't want to leave. But I felt that I had to go back, since I never said goodbye to Nadine. I felt that I was obligated to go back. After to returning to Nadine's I felt so unhappy I kept thinking about Noreen and her sisters… how kind and nice they were to me. My physical body was at Nadine's but my mind and heart were at Noreen's.

After a few weeks, I went to visit Noreen and Vicky again. This time their other sister Fiona was there as well. Fiona was still living in Uganda with her husband and her family. Fiona came to visit her sisters often. After spending time with these women, I saw how pleasant all of them were, and I made the decision to go and live with them. Even though I had lost most of my trust in people, I figured nothing could be worse than living with Nadine and her sister, so, Noreen's would become my new home.

I went back home and announced to Nadine that I was going to live with Noreen. I told her that I was going to move the following weekend. I knew this would give me time to gather all my stuff together. She didn't say a word. I think in Nadine's mind, she thought if she didn't comment or say anything that would stop me from leaving.

That Friday, I did all my laundry and packed all my belongings. The next day, I left to live with Noreen and Vicky. The day I left, Nadine's sister was not home, and Dative had gone to visit some of her friends, apparently, Nadine had to sleep in the house all by herself. Later, Nadine complained to my brother Damascene that I had left without saying goodbye and a lot of other lies about me and my exit. She accused me of being ungrateful. Looking back on that situation, I am so glad I had the courage to leave that house.

Since I was the youngest, Vicky and Noreen spoiled me and helped me forget the nightmares that I had been dealing with. Noreen loved me. She even went with me sometimes to visit my sister's friend Julienne. Noreen and Vicky would look at me and cry—they couldn't believe most of our family members had been killed and they never got a chance to meet some of them. When Noreen talked about Nkubili, she cried. She was such a loving and compassionate person. Vicky was a devout born-again Christian. Every night she prayed for me, I think it was the first time I heard anyone praying in tongues face-to-face. She really made a big difference in my life even though I never went to church with her.

Since Vicky grew up in Uganda, she didn't speak much Kinyarwanda. She prayed in Ruganda (one of the language they speak in Uganda). I couldn't understand what she was saying. She read her Bible every day. In the night, she would go in the room and sing, pray, and sometimes still cry. I didn't understand any of it but I could feel its power.

Vicky and I did the house chores together, even though she didn't let me do much, and after we were finished, we would go into the city to walk around and stop in the different shops. Vicky and I stayed home while Noreen went to work. For the first time since my sister left, I felt I had a family again. I was so grateful.

Sadly, all that fun and love didn't last long. Suddenly, it was time to go to the boarding school. I really didn't want to leave them. I was dreading returning to my hometown. While I lived at Nadine's, I couldn't wait for the school to start so I can leave her house but it was different now. At Noreen's, I didn't want to leave the comfort and love that now surrounded me. Noreen bought me a lot of supplies to take to school. They told me that they would come to visit me. My brother Damascene came to take me to school.

Before I went to school, I wanted to go visit my hometown for some closure. I told my brother that I wanted to pass by where my parents used to live. Damascene tried to talk me out of it because he didn't want to go there; but I didn't budge. My brother stated that if we went there we wouldn't be able to find another vehicle to take me to school; trying to discourage me from going there. The school was in the middle of nowhere. No vehicle went there except if you had rented a motorcycle or a cab in Butare. There was no other way to get to the school except by foot. I told my brother that I didn't care if we had to walk all day as long, as I was able to see where our parents used to live.

From Kigali, Damascene and I went straight to Butare, from Butare to Munini, which was my hometown. We got to our hometown in the early afternoon. When we got there, we went straight to visit my cousin Alexia, Tim's wife. Tim was not there. Rumor had it that Tim and Alexia had marital problems after genocide and Tim moved away. After we sat there for a while, I told Damascene and Alexia that I was going to see the place where our house used to be. My brother declined to go with me but he wished me luck. He told me that he would like to keep the memory he had when my parents were still there and didn't want to ruin his own memory. So, I walked there alone. When I got there, I could tell where our house used to be because the flowers were still there. There was nothing else besides bushes and those overgrown flowers. I sat there for about two hours by myself and couldn't imagine how after one year, things could vanish like there had been nothing there before. I sat there looking at the sunset and spent time reflecting on our lives there. I remember how that sunset used to give me such excitement. We would sit in our driveway and look at it. The sounds of children laughing playing nearby, crying children, the voices of my cousins, my uncles, my aunts, my mom, my precious mom, my dad, so sweet and strong. How I missed them terribly. That joy was replaced with sorrow deep in my heart. When I couldn't take that overwhelming and excruciating pain deep in my heart, I got up and walked back to Alexia's house.

By the time I returned, it started to get dark outside. We were not able to go to my school that day, since it was so far away. We slept at my cousin's house and then got up early the next morning to go to school. I had no idea how far I would have to walk. I used to be able to see the school, from my house, especially at night. You could see the lights peeking in the top of the building in the faraway mountains. Those lights seemed so close, but I had no idea how far away the school was.

Chapter 17

"When times are good be happy, but when times are bad, consider: God has made the one as well as the other. Therefore, a man cannot discover his future."

Ecclesiastes 8:14

We got up early in the morning; we walked and walked for hours. At some point, I felt that I could not take another footstep. I was unable to even count how much time I sat down. My poor brother Damascene, I kept dragging behind him. By the time we got there I couldn't walk any further. I had bruises between my thighs. There were times I couldn't even walk and I would just sit down, and my brother would just stand there and watch me in disbelief. One time we got to this little river you had to walk through, there was no bridge to cross over; and I told my brother that there was no way I was going to take off my shoes and walk through that water. I didn't even have the strength to take off my shoes.

Damascene took the suitcase he was carrying to the other side of the river, and then came back and carried me across. I think at that point he just pitied me or he didn't have energy to argue with me. To this day, Damascene still teases me about how he carried me across the river. When we arrived at school it was lunchtime, and I had to register and get a school ID. They assigned a student to show me the dorms. After my brother dropped me off at the dorm, he left. I didn't want him to leave. I wanted to tell him that I didn't want to stay there by myself. I was petrified. I felt as if all the girls were staring at me. However, one of the girls was nice and told me to change into my uniform, so I could go eat with them. I was in my regular clothes, I had to change into the uniform, a khaki skirt and a white blouse or T-shirt. I changed and went with her.

Honestly, I really didn't want to go anywhere; the only thing I really wanted to do was just go to bed. I was so exhausted and didn't care much about food, even though I was starving. When I got in the cafeteria I saw a couple of people I knew from my childhood. Andre was there, the one I lived with at Zone Turquoise with the French soldiers after I got rescued during genocide. Also, Innocent, my childhood friend, and one girl named Phina, who told me she was from the area near where my parents lived before the genocide. I realized that it was not going to be that bad after all. Phina had a best friend named Clemantine which she introduced me to; I hit it off with her right away. Finally, I no longer felt alone or afraid.

Phina and Innocent were in their third school year, Clemantine was in her fifth year, Andre was in the sixth, which was his last year, and I was in my first year. Thus, I had a lot of people who were protecting me since the freshmen were always picked on. Phina, Clemantine, Innocent, and I bonded more. We cried with one another when we talked about the genocide and our lost family members. Each one of us had experienced a different yet unique story. We shared a lot but I am sure we all had some secret we didn't have enough guts to tell each other about. For instance, I never told anyone that I was raped during the genocide. After the genocide, if you were raped, you were not allowed to talk about it. People looked down on you, as though it was your fault. You were considered filthy; nobody wanted to have anything to do with you. This is still the attitude of some people, I am sure.

Phina and Innocent were living in the orphanage because they didn't have any other place to go and they were too young to live on their own. I was so thankful that at least I still had a sister who could take care of me and worry about me even if she was no longer around. Innocent had a little brother and a sister who were living with him at the orphanage. He was always sad and worried that he was not old enough to take care of his siblings. His case was common in Rwanda after the genocide. A lot of kids found themselves alone without an adult to look after them. There were a lot of kids raising other kids as well. Also, there were older women and men who were left with no children, or left without their husbands or wives. It always made me sad yet at the same time grateful to the family that I had. I couldn't imagine if I had to live alone with my three nieces without my older sister. What would I have done?

———

Several weeks into the semester, a girl named Jeanette arrived at school late. Jeanette was from Kigali as well. I didn't know how she ended up at that school. I was so glad she came. She became my best friend. However, by the time Jeanette came there, I didn't have anything left. The girls I lived with had stolen everything I had, including my underwear, my Kotex and all my money. I was so naïve when I got there. I would forget to lock my suitcase or at other times I would leave money in the pocket of my shorts laying on the top of my bed. Usually when I got back, everything would be gone. These girls could steal anything; I couldn't believe how one can still someone's undergarments and wear them. You would think after what I had been through I would be smart and take care of my stuff. People just don't learn. So, when Jeanette got there, I told her what had happened to me and warned her to lock and guard her stuff carefully. Jeanette was so sweet. She shared all her stuff since there were no shops near the school.

I will never forget the time I spent at that school. There was pain, suffering and healing, all at the same time. Most of the kids who were there were living in the orphanage and many were severely depressed, a lot of them had I believe was Posttraumatic Stress Disorder, although I didn't know what it was that time. We seemed to get melancholy at the same time. It was like a contagious disease. We would sit and cry and talk about the genocide. This time was distressing, but at the same time, comforting. This time was very precious to me because I had people my age who were facing a similar pain to mine. We all had a different story yet they seemed to be similar at the same time. Here we all were: children who didn't have any parents or any adults to explain to us what had happened. We had nobody to teach us how we could deal with all the pain we were facing. We were left to figure it all on out our own. Since no one was old enough to understand we just sat there, holding our hands, hanging our heads and crying. As simple as that was – this time we cried together helped all of us to cope somehow.

Also, I remember this little girl. I am calling her a little girl, even though she probably was the same age as I was. She was so skinny; I was much bigger. The little girl looked too young to be in high school. Her name was Francine. Francine really loved me and wanted to sleep in my bed because she was too afraid to sleep alone. However, there was a problem of wetting the bed, which I didn't know about. Later… the first time she slept with me, Francine peed on my bed.

In the morning, my mattress was soaked, causing me to wake up smelling like pee. Consequently, I was mad at her. Francine apologized and promised she would never do it again. She insisted it happened because she drank too much tea the night before in the cafeteria. I made her wash my sheets and we took my mattress outside so it would dry. The next day she begged me to let her sleep with me again. That night she didn't pee on me, but the next night I was covered with pee once again. I felt so bad for her. I found it so hard to say 'no' to her so every day that we slept in the same bed, I woke up in a pool of pee. I think maybe because I had once had a little sister, I felt compassion toward her. Plus, it broke my heart when other girls in our dorm made fun of her. I didn't have the heart to say *no*; her fear of sleeping alone seemed genuine. Who knows what have happened to her, too, because she was still urinating in the bed, even at her age.

When Jeanette came along, I was so happy. I slept in her bed to avoid sleeping with Francine. My mattress had stains all over it... to the point I was so disgusted and could no longer bare to sleep on it. I realized she had a problem, and I felt sorry for her. Since I could not help her but was enabling by letting her to keep peeing on me I decided to never go back into that bed. The other girls would make fun of her and thought I was too nice because I let her sleep with me. I really wanted to help her, but the poor girl couldn't help it. Sometimes Francine would ask if she could sleep in my bed, even though I was not sleeping in it. She told me that it made her feel less alone, because she imagined that I was there. I told her to go for it but I never slept in that bed again. And she kept sleeping in my bed.

I lived at that school for three months. Then unexpectedly my brother Damascene arrived and told me that I had to pack my stuff and go with him. I thought that maybe I was about to get transferred to the other school. He told me that my sister Christina needed me to go see her in Nairobi. I was so excited and couldn't believe that finally I would see my sister again. She finally proved everyone wrong, I thought to myself. I packed only some of my clothes and donated all my uniforms and school supplies to the girls. I was sad to leave Jeanette there by herself. We had bonded like sisters in those few months. I gave her my favorite dress, and she gave me hers so we would not forget each other. We said goodbye and cried. Then I continued my journey not knowing where I was going to end up.

———————

My brother and I got a ride to Butare and from Butare to Kigali, we took a taxi. When I got to Kigali, I went to see Noreen and Vicky to tell them I was heading to Nairobi. The next day, it became time to visit my sister's friend Julienne who gave me instructions on how to get to my sister. Julienne told me to take a bus to Kampala in Uganda, and from Kampala, I would meet Margaret – one my sister's sisters-in-law, who would lead the way.

After a couple of days, Damascene and Julienne's sister Letitia took me to the bus station and I got into the bus heading to Kampala. Although I have seen Margaret a long time ago at my sister's wedding, I really didn't remember her. I had no idea how in the world I was going to recognize her. I really did not think she'd remember me either. Additionally, I didn't speak English or Ruganda. Therefore, I was wondering what I was going to do if we missed each other. I was anxious about going to another country where I didn't know anyone.

When we got to the border of Rwanda and Uganda, we had to get out of the bus to present our travel papers. The border patrol guards searched the bus to see if there was anyone or anything that shouldn't be leaving the country. Before I left Rwanda, Julienne told me that if anyone asked me where I was going when we got to the border that I should say I was going to visit my aunt who lived in Kampala. At that time, people were going in and out of Uganda like it was another town in Rwanda because now people were free to go there.

So, Julienne didn't think it should be a problem for me to say that I was visiting an aunt in Uganda. When the officer at the border asked where I was going, I told him what Julienne had told me to say. He asked if I had been there before, and I told him no. He also asked me if I spoke English or Ruganda and I told him that I spoke neither language. He was very nice; and then told me to have a nice trip.

While I was having my conversation with that officer there was a young man sitting behind me who was listening to us. He didn't say a word. I had seen him on the same bus sitting and talking with a girl the whole way. The girl eventually got off the bus. When she left, the man came and talked to me. He said, "So you are going to Uganda and you don't know anyone there?"

I nodded my head, "Yes." He also asked me if I knew who was coming to pick me up. I told him not really. We talked some more and he told me that he was enrolled in school at the National University of Rwanda and was going home to visit his family since they were still living in Uganda. After this conversation, he went back to his seat and I went to mine.

———————

The bus ride to Kampala was long, close to eight hours. I was sick the whole trip and wanted to throw up because of the smell of the bus. I always got car sick upon entering a bus. I don't know if it is the gas they used or if there were too much people with different odors in the bus. Finally, we reached Kampala. I was so nervous; a lot of questions were going through my head. "What if Margaret didn't come to get me, or we missed each other, what am I going to do or how am I going to sleep?"

When the bus stopped, I let everyone else get out and I stayed behind. I looked around and when I saw there was no one left on the bus, I started to get up and go. When I looked behind once more I noticed that the guy I had talked to earlier was still on the bus as well. Eventually, the two of us got out at the same time.

Just as I was about to put my feet on the ground, I saw Margaret and recognized her right away. She recognized me as well. She came running, hugging me, and crying at the same time. Margaret was so affectionate. The man from the bus was still behind me. He said hello to Margaret and introduced himself as Justin. Justin told her that the reason he waited in the bus was to make sure I was safe. Justin told us that he didn't want me to get lost and that he was going to ask if he could take me to his family's house if I didn't have anyone waiting for me. We thanked him, and Margaret told him the name of the hotel where we were staying that night.

Later in the evening, Justin came back to visit us with his brother. I remember hearing them vaguely because I was sleeping. I heard Justin's brother telling Margaret that he went to Makerere University in Uganda. Also, I heard them exchanging addresses but that was all; I was so tired that I went right to sleep. Now, I regret it. I wish I had had a chance to thank him.

The next day early in the morning Margaret and I got up and went to take the bus to Nairobi. I don't remember much about the ride except that it was an even longer ride than the one from Kigali to Kampala. We got there in the late afternoon and took a taxi to where my sister Christina and her sisters-in-law were staying. Even though I was tired, when I saw my sister and my nieces, my exhaustion disappeared. For the first time in a year we were all seeing one another. We sat and talked and got caught up on the things that had happened to me while she was gone.

I had never told her anything before, because I didn't want to worry her. After all, she had had enough to deal with her own. Christina told me why she wanted me to come immediately. She and the girls had been granted asylum to the United States. When they passed the interview, my sister told them that she had a dependent little sister who survived the genocide and had no one to care for her and asked if I could come as well. The officer told them to bring me as soon as possible. At last, I was united with my family and there was nothing that was going to separate us ever again.

———

A few days later, Margaret and my sister took me for an interview at American embassy in Nairobi. Margaret was the only person who spoke English. She came to interpret for us. When I got to the office,

Margaret sat next to me with the Immigration officer in front of us. The officer asked questions about the genocide and what had happened and how I had managed to survive. It was then that I think I cried for the first time, after a stranger asked me to retell my story.

By the time I was done, Margaret and the officer were sobbing. To tell you the truth, I don't even remember what I told them to make them cry like that. Because in the middle of interview the lady who was doing the interview told me to stop and that she had gathered enough information. Little did they know that I hadn't told them everything.

The officer sympathized with me for having gone through all those horrible experiences at such a young age. Then she called someone to come down to sign my acceptance papers to the United States. Usually in order to be told that you passed the interview, you had to go through two interviews. I think this lady saw that I had had enough and decided to fast-track my approval. Here colleague didn't ask any questions. He just had a sad look on his face. Margaret couldn't believe how smooth my interview went because usually the interviewers gave people such a hard time.

After that, we went back to where we were living. We stayed in Kenya for two months after the interview. Even though the interview was over, it took a long process for people to get ready to leave. You had to go for a physical checkup and blood tests for all sorts of diseases. By the time you left for the US, it was months later.

———

At that time, my sister was living with one of her other sisters-in-law and her four children. The sister-in-law's family had an opportunity to go to Europe. Now it would not have made sense to keep paying for the big house we were living in; besides, their landlord had become hostile. She once called the police on us. I am not sure what the story was but they took all of us to the police station and we were there for a long time until Margaret came. She probably had to give them money to let us go. During that same time, Margaret was living on campus where she was going to school. There she had a little room, and there was no way she could put all of us in her dorm room. She always had a lot on her shoulders; Margaret was constantly hosting people. Now that I think about it, I wonder how she was able to study. There were always problems, one right after another.

But, somehow, she always found a way to keep all of us safe. She was in her twenties, but she had responsibilities no one could handle. Sometimes, I wonder if we ever really thanked her for all the things she did for all of us. Personally, I am deeply grateful for everything Margaret did. I am sure God will reward her, what no one could be able to give her.

As the sister-in-law and her children waited to fly out, they moved in with a Kenyan family that was good friends with Margaret and had became a great support for her and the whole family. My sister, my three nieces and I moved in with another Kenyan family. They provided us with one bedroom to share. The first couple of weeks we were there, this family was happy, but then as the days went by, the woman of the house became cold. Up to this day, I don't know what we did to her. Since there were so many of us, Margaret made sure we had money to buy groceries so they would not feel that they had to feed us. Also, everyone made sure we did all chores around the house. Most of days the family were gone to work or school, and my sister and I cleaned and cooked meals for everyone.

I can never forget the day the rain fell on my sister and I on our way back from grocery shopping. We were carrying paper bags full of groceries. All the paper bags got wet and the groceries fell on the ground. As we were running behind to catch a Matatu (taxis in Nairobi); most of the groceries fell on the ground. Trying to pick up everything from the wet ground and the hard-pouring rain on our back was something I could never forget. And trying to hold semi-left groceries in the broken wet paper bags in our arms was an unwinnable game. The sugar and salt we bought that day had all melted. By the time we got home we were soaking wet and more than half of the groceries were ruined.

The Kenyan woman we lived with was a control freak. All of the children, who were university students at that time, were terrified of her. My sister and I cleaned and cooked, but nothing seemed to satisfy that woman. No matter what we did, she was never happy with us. We lived there about three weeks until the lady got so mad and then she kicked us out of her house. We were confused and didn't understand how a person could invite someone to come stay with them and then in the end decide to kick them out. What was the point of inviting us into her home if in end she was going to kick us out?

However, while we were living with this Kenyan family, there was a man from Rwanda who often came to visit her. The man, for unknown reasons, was afraid to go back to Rwanda and he never really said why. I always thought to myself maybe he had committed acts of genocide. At that time there were a lot of genocidaires who were fugitives in Kenya. He also hated the RPF. For some odd reason, every time he left this woman's house from his visit, the lady was mad. I don't know if he made up some stories to tell our host so she would kick us out of her house. I remember one day she was so angry at me. She accused me of calling her an old lady in my language and claimed that she heard me talking about her. This outburst came right after that man left. It seemed like every time that Rwandan man visited and then left, the woman was angrier.

After we got kicked out, the only place Margaret had left to put us in was her dorm room. We went to live with her in her little small bedroom that had a twin bed in it. One of her friends was on vacation at the time; Margaret asked her if we could use her room while she was trying to figure out where to put us. My sister and my three nieces went and packed themselves in Margaret's friend's room, and I slept in Margaret's room.

Luckily, we got kicked out of that lady's house the same time Margaret's sister and her family left. When their hosts found out what happened and that Margaret had all of us on the campus, they insisted that we move in with them. This Kenyan family hosted every single one of Margaret's' relatives. I don't think there is anyone who came here to the United States or somewhere else, without first living with this family. The couple' names were Robert and Sonia Mwadime. The Mwadimes were a blessing from God. They were born again Christians, who you really could say were examples of true Christianity. They loved people and God; there are not enough words to describe them. At that time, there was one niece Emma and nephew Aloys of Margaret's who were already living with this family as well, and they still they agreed to take five more people on top of that.

About a week after I moved to Mwandimes, I had an emotional breakdown. I think my mind was so overwhelmed to the point I couldn't hold it all in any longer. Perhaps it was the Holy Spirit living in Mwadimes' home. The whole week I cried nonstop — I cried about everything, the abuse I went through during genocide and never had a chance to process, many of my tears were for my family that I never had time to mourn because I was trying to save my life. I remembered the day those people killed my mother and my little brother Augustin and my little sister Sylvie. Also, I remembered and could hear in my mind the sound of all the grenades and guns roaring that poured to my family on that day. In the end, I felt that my soul died with my mother and wondered if I would ever be the same. There was this horrible picture cemented in my mind of my mother lying on the ground naked because those horrible people took her clothes after they killed her; this is what they did to everybody. They were stripped after being killed.

I sobbed as I thought about how I never even had a chance to bury my own parents and would never know where their remains were. Knowing the horror they went through caused me to feel so much rage and bitterness and hatred.

No one could soothe me during that week. Emma just stared at me and would from time to time just sit next to me in silence, and sometimes, Emma would say, "Anamaliya, it's okay! You will be okay!" I didn't eat nor drink. I wept non-stop night and day for a whole week. Thinking about all my family and my friends and the fact that I never got a chance to say bye to them. Everyone felt helpless.

In the end, Sonia sat me down one night and prayed for me. She said that I didn't have to be sad and alone because Jesus died on the cross for me, and if I told him how I felt, He would take all my pain and the sadness away. She read me Bible verses and told me that Jesus loved me before I was born because he knew I would need Him to take all this pain from me.

However, she told me that Jesus wouldn't force Himself into my life, that I would need to let Him come into my heart. That was the first time I heard someone telling me anything like that. Even though I lived with the couple during the genocide who told me about God and how He could protect me, they never explained Jesus the way Sonia did. This was different. Jesus was someone who loved me enough to die on the cross just for me, someone who could take my pain and sins away.

I felt overwhelmed, and wanted to know this God personally who could take all our inside pain away. Sonia led me through a prayer, after she was done praying for me and for the first time, I felt relieved. Now, I felt as though the weight that were in my heart and mind had been lifted. She prayed for me some more and gave me verses in the Bible that I could read for myself. After a couple of days of praying and reading the Bible with me, she told me that to heal completely I had to let go and forgive all those people who had killed my family and who had hurt me and many others. Sonia gave me a gift of lifetime and she has no idea the impact she made in my life. Now, as I sit here writing this, I believe with all my heart that's what God intended for me to pass Sonia and the Mwadime home for this very reason to be introduced to His Mighty salvation. Being kicked out of that Kenyan woman's home turned out to be the best gift. Everything happens in our lives - good or bad, God has a last say in it and He is intentional.

My best memory was when Sonia and her husband took me to church. This was the first time I had ever attended a Pentecostal church. Even though, I have had few encounters with people who told me about God through all my life and I knew in my heart that He was the one who has saved me. I also can surely say that I have been touched by His hand during genocide at that Seventh-Day Adventist couple's home. However, I never truly experienced the presence of God myself in a church setting. I felt God's peace covering all my being. And I remember closing my eyes and tears streaming down all over my cheeks; and these tears were tears of joy and I didn't care about my crying in the middle of a thousand strangers. I just felt the hand of God touching me. I couldn't believe how much God loved me. The church was huge with thousands of people, singing, praying, and raising their hands. Even though I didn't understand the language and the songs they were singing but I remember being mesmerized by the Holy Spirit at work in that service. After that first service, I couldn't wait for Sunday to come so I could go back. When I was there I longed to stay there. I didn't want to leave.

When I was in that church I felt the assurance of God that I no longer have to deal with the pain of losing my family alone. I was also hopeful that I would see them again in heaven.

We lived with the Mwadimes about three weeks and then headed to the United States. When we were leaving, Sonia gave me a Bible and wrote a message that always turns me around when I'm not on the right path. The message said, "My dearest, in the short time we have known you, we have loved you very much. But God loves you more and He has always known you. Live for Him all your days and He will never leave you nor forsake you."

Through Sonia's help by introducing me to the love of God, I decided to give most of my pain to God. And now I am so glad that I did. Through life challenges, experience, education, and more maturity, I came to understand that bitterness destroys the person who carries it. It takes the grace of God to forgive the Hutus for what they did to us. I truly pray that someday we will let the pain, hate, bitterness, and anger we carry in our hearts go and move toward forgiving the people who destroyed our lives. It is my belief that if we could forgive them whole heartedly we could all be healed. We need this for our own sake and the sake of the generations that will come after us.

After the genocide, as people began to account for the crimes committed there was a lot of bitterness and fighting between many genocide survivors and bystanders. After the genocide, some people testified against those who hid them and had them put in jail. I am not saying that all the people told the truth, but you never really know what happened to people during the genocide. For example, in my case, Tim and Bubba did what they could to save my life but it doesn't take away from what they did to me either. Just because I never testified against them doesn't mean they were innocent. If I had not felt that love and forgiveness from God, I don't think I could have forgiven them either.

Some people also looked down on other people who got raped during genocide. One of my acquaintances from Rwanda was talking about women who got raped during the genocide and the HIV/AIDS that resulted from it. I don't remember what she was saying, but I looked at her and I said, "What if I was raped?" She turned to me and said, "If you were raped during the genocide, you must never tell anyone because most people remain single. No one wants to marry them." I didn't say anything more. But, this conversation stuck with me. I couldn't believe how people could be so ignorant.

How could you reject people because of what happened to them in the past? I know this woman loves genocide survivors, and she would do anything for them. So, the level of ignorance was surprising. It hurt me that people were expected to go around with that much pain and yet had never been given space to talk about it, especially because it would jeopardize their chance of being married. Why would these people care if I got married or not? At least I would have peace of mind. What kind of man would not accept me because of my painful past? I don't need that kind of man. We were the victims, but still we were made to feel as though we had chosen to be raped. And if our brothers and sisters could not accept our broken souls, who would— the people who took the joy and our innocence from us?

I realized that people needed to be educated to see beyond their ignorance, to understand that there was nothing wrong with these women. Instead of casting them away, they needed to be embraced and given extra tender loving care, because they had been violated in a place no one could ever reach except God. I still believe that together, as Rwandans, we can make this happen and see the healing take place.

There is no human who could do it without the power of God's help. Without God's help, how could you forgive people who killed all your family, raped you and left you emotionally dead by taking your innocence and purity? Regardless of what these wrongdoers did to us, we need to forgive them in order to live a better life. By carrying this bitterness inside of us, it just gives them too much power. The better way to live is to forgive them and then continue living to the fullest. I came to realize that bitterness and hatred can destroy lives while the people you hate may live in harmony. Only forgiving heals people and I don't know how much I can say this. We deserve to be happy and live our lives to the fullest of our potential.

PART IV: Exodus
Chapter 18

*"Have I not commanded you? Be strong
and courageous. Do not be terrified; do not be
discouraged, for the Lord your God will be with
you wherever you go."*

~ Joshua 1:9

The flight to the United States was long and exhausting. We stopped in Germany and then again in New York. When we got to New York, we waited there for a long time. I think our layover was six or seven hours, because they couldn't find a flight connecting us to New Hampshire that day. We sat at that airport for hours waiting for them to find us another flight. While we were waiting at the New York airport, one of my nieces Aurore got real tired and hungry. Aurore was five years old at that time and was whining that she wanted food. I was joking with her by saying, "You know, Aurore, if you dance for these people maybe they could give you the money, and then we could buy food."

She started dancing; it was very funny, and to this day, we tease her about how she danced that day for food in New York. Unfortunately, no one gave her money, just a few smiles.

Finally, around midnight, they found us a connection that would leave the following day. They gave us a hotel room for an overnight stay. We were all so completely worn out that we crashed the minute we got into our room. I remember that a worker from the hotel brought us food after we got there, and I did not even try it. My sister and nieces could not eat either. When the guy came back to pick up trays and realized that we did not touch the food, first he sat down on my bed and tried to feed me, and when I refused, he started eating the food. As he was consuming our food, he tried to have little chat and encouraged us to come and join him; even though no one understood anything he was saying. We were not interested because of our fatigue. The next day we thought it was bizarre how he sat there and ate all the food.

Early the next morning, they came to take us to the airport to catch a flight to New Hampshire. The guy who came to pick us up was so loud and talked too much that morning and I was wondering how a person could be that loud that early. We all were staring at him and smiling because most of us didn't have a clue what he was saying, and I could see Christina was concentrating on figuring out what the guy was saying. The guy gave up and started to pick up our baggage and then we got it. We all were still exhausted and jetlagged, even the little English my sister spoke was not coming out easily.

When we got to the airport in Manchester, New Hampshire my sister's family-in-law were waiting for us. They had come with some of our sponsors from Dover's Quaker organization. After we had been granted asylum, the person who invited you had to find a sponsor who would help you settle into life in the US for the first couple of months after arrival. We were sponsored by a Quaker couple named Dick and Jane. Dick was a physicist and professor at the state university, and his wife was an artist and worked at home. We drove about an hour to get to Jane and Dick's. They lived in a small college town, in the faculty neighborhood.

When we arrived, I couldn't believe we were in America. The wooden house was built in the middle of bushes. Even though I didn't tell anyone, I was pretty disappointed. For some reason, I thought we were in the wrong country. I couldn't believe this was America. I had only known Americans through the depictions of American life in films. I thought the whole country is like New York or Los Angeles. So, when we ended up in the small town of Durham, New Hampshire, it was drastically different.

We hit it off right away with Jane and Dick. The first weeks that they had been meant to host us turned into two months. Oddly enough, Jane was born the same year as our mother, and her husband was born the same year as our father. They became our family.

When we got to the States, I didn't speak a word of English. Jane made it her mission to teach me English and in her own creative way. If you came to her house when we lived there – everything in the house had labels on them, the floor, the ceiling, the walls, the cabinets, and everything inside of them.

She was my teacher, my friend, and at times, she seemed like my mother. Even if I couldn't have a conversation with her, it didn't stop Jane from taking me shopping, to the movies, and museums. When we moved to our apartment, she came to visit us every day. We had a day for shopping, one for reading, and another for going to the movies. She treated me like her own. She yelled at me when I didn't clean my room, and she praised me when I did well. We developed a strong love and bond over those early months that would turn into years of friendship

Chapter 19

"I will go before you and will level the mountains; I will break down gates of bronze and cut through bars of iron. I will give you hidden treasures, riches stored in secret places, so that you may know that I am the LORD, the God of Israel, who summons you by name."

~ *Isaiah 45:2-3 NIV*

During the transitional period of my life – getting used to living in the United States – I remember spending most of my time in bed. I was always crying, even if I didn't know why I was crying. Sometimes, I even cried when my sister and my nieces were not home, because I always had the fear of losing them. When they left to go somewhere my mind would race with all the terrible things that could happen to them. At night, I couldn't sleep and when other people were sleeping, I would cry in my bed.

In that first year, I felt very insecure and didn't want anyone to know. Even my own sister did not know about all the things I endured during the genocide until about two years after we had been in the US. I had so many insecurities that I carried because of my past. I had low self-esteem and thought I was ugly. I hated myself, and if people told me that I was beautiful, I always felt that they were just feeling sorry for me because I was unattractive. I thought they could see through me and that they were able to see what had happened to me in the past.

Even when I laughed, I was always a wreck on the inside. I had so much insecurity I didn't think anyone would ever want me or love me. On my worst day, I could still sense the odor of Bubba. All I did during this period of time was get up, go to school, come home, eat and sleep. On weekends, I just slept and spent most of my time at home.

My misery continued until three teenagers from Rwanda moved to New Hampshire for school, two boys and a girl that were my age. Their names were Olivia, Liam, and Jaxon and they were all siblings. Olivia and I became fast friends. We were like magnets — always attached to one another. I was so pleased to have friends who were my age and spoke my language. My loneliness and depression ended and was instead replaced with teenage mischief.

It was with them that I went to a nightclub for the first time. I got a boyfriend and stopped going to church. The same way I used to get excited for the church on Sundays, I began to get excited for Thursday and Friday and going to dance clubs. My praying stopped. With my new friends, I didn't need God in my life anymore. At the time, I didn't realize that I could have both Him and friends and be even happier.

Having friends made the rest of my high school years much more bearable. No day went by without me seeing Olivia – though she always got me in trouble with my sister. Olivia and I were still under twenty-one but we always found IDs to get into the night clubs. There even were times I used Olivia's ID. She would use her passport and give me her driver's license. Olivia was a couple of months older than I was.

One day, we went to a local Mexican restaurant. The place was crowded so they wanted to sit us at the bar. Although I didn't drink, I still needed to show an ID. Since I was still under age, Olivia gave the waitress her ID, and then she handed it back to me under the table while the waitress was still looking at Liam's ID. She came to me and I handed her the same ID that Olivia had just given her. I was shaking, but Olivia was fearless. The waitress didn't even notice, and up to this day I never understood how we never got caught.

My sister didn't approve of my new and risky behavior. I didn't go to church anymore, and every Friday and Saturday I went clubbing. Sometimes we went to Boston to go dancing. On top of that, I got a boyfriend, against my sister's will and God's will, too. There was a point I thought I was going overboard and wanted to stop, but Olivia and I were inseparable. I couldn't just let go and stop hanging out with her. People thought we were sisters. If one of us was not at a certain place, people would ask the other, "Where is your sister?"

I remember one time I told my sister that I was going to sleep at Olivia's house. Olivia and I ended up going clubbing in Boston instead. We spent the night at our friends' house in Boston. Olivia always had crazy ideas, and she was so spontaneous. The night we went to Boston I felt guilty about lying to my sister. Around seven in the morning, I told Olivia to get up and go home. We drove back home, and took showers and went to church. When my sister saw us, she was so happy. She may have thought we had some kind of revelation and were going to change our ways. Throughout the service, I was so convicted that I decided I needed to stop being rebellious. From then on, I tried to change. Constantly fighting with my sister wasn't worth it. Olivia and I now had a reputation as "bad girls". Most of the things people were saying were wrong assumptions but we certainly didn't give them any reason to think otherwise. Even though we were going clubbing regularly, neither one of us got drunk or picked up guys. We just went to the clubs to dance, and after we were done dancing, we went home. Sometimes Olivia and I didn't even go anywhere. We would sit in the car outside of the house for hours talking nonsense.

———

With all the distraction from my new friendships, my grades had been slipping. One day it hit me that I might not be able to get into college because my GPA was low. I went and cried to my guidance counselor. She told me not to worry because she was going to do everything in her power to get me into a school. Everything was new to me and my sister, we didn't know anything about the college application - such as applying for colleges, visiting schools, etc.

My guidance counselor came to my rescue. She asked the principal if she could take a day off and take me to visit colleges; and he agreed. She made appointments to go visit schools. We visited several schools in three nearby states. By the time we got to the last state, it was late and we stayed in the hotel so we could continue with our tours the next day.

The following day, we visited St. Joseph College, which was a small women's college in Connecticut. I loved the school the moment I saw it and knew that I was going to go there. Since I wanted to change my life, I felt that going to this school would help me get my grades up again without much distraction.

At the end of my senior year in high school, I started calming down. I began to let go off a lot of things. I was still dating my boyfriend and pretending that I enjoyed church. I stopped going to nightclubs because I didn't want to fight with my sister anymore.

After my senior year, I went to St. Joseph College as planned. I really wanted to redeem my life and get serious with my education. When I got at St. Joseph's though, I didn't really like the school. There was no big difference between going there and going to a coed school. They did the same things, including drugs in their dorms and bringing guys over. The worst part was that I missed my family so much. Every time I called home and I heard them laughing, I cried because I wanted to be with them.

Every other week I went home. I was broke all of the time because all the money I made at school ended up being used for bus tickets. By the end of the first semester, I knew that I was not going to return. I went home for Christmas break, and after it was over, I was closer to my family and didn't want to live far away from them anymore. So, during the spring semester, I applied to transfer to the University of New Hampshire, where I was accepted, for my sophomore year. Going away made me appreciate my family more, and I valued their love more than ever.

I can never be far from my family. One of my friends even said that when I arrived in Rwanda in 2003, at the airport in Kigali, I called my sister to come pick me up, without thinking that she was not there. I cannot see how I could live without my Christina or my nieces. My nieces were braver than I could ever be. They all went their separate ways to colleges and no one failed and came back like me.

When I came back home and went to University of New Hampshire, I was happy for several months. But after a while there was nothing to motivate me. Some days were better than others, though, there were times when I didn't even want to go to class because I didn't see the point of continuing my education. I prayed to God and knew that He had delivered me from all those feelings of doubt and would still give me peace of mind. I always had to keep reminding myself that there was no need to feel this way. But still these feeling always crawled back in my heart and continued to darken my days.

Chapter 20

"Train a child in the way he should go, and when he is old he will not turn from it."

~ Proverbs 22:6

While I was working at Walmart, a lady came to my register and asked me where I was from. I told her that I was from Rwanda. She said to me, "Child, how did you survive or were you here when that tragedy happened?" I explained that I was in Rwanda when it happened. She asked about my parents and I told her that they were both killed during the genocide. The woman then said to me, "Get married and have children." I didn't understand what she was talking about. In my mind, I wondered what marriage and kids had to do with happiness. However, that thought stuck in my mind and I started to believe that maybe if I found the right guy and married him that would take away the loneliness I felt. I thought maybe when you got married and had kids; thinking about yourself goes away because you become absorbed in the lives of your children or in the relationship. Or maybe there is a love and happiness that comes with having children.

I remembered how my mom loved all of us. The love she had for my siblings and me, I could never explain to someone. My mom grew up with no relatives. Her mother died after giving birth to her, and her father died while she was quite young, making it impossible for her to remember both of them. She had an older brother who later also died after he had three children. Her maternal grandparent raised her. Mom used to tell us how growing up she was spoiled by her grandparents, but was hated by her uncles because they were jealous of her.

However, even though her grandparents loved her, mom was always lonely because she had no siblings. And I remembered how she had told me that she got saved by her children. I never understood what she meant until that woman's comment got me thinking about it again. I remembered how we were the center of her life. Mom loved us so much. She taught us to make decisions and instilled us in the importance of family. At the time, I thought she was crazy. Why was she telling us those things as if she was going somewhere? I think because Mom grew up alone, she was afraid that she might die and we could go through the same thing.

I also think Mom had that fear that if something happened to her we wouldn't have anywhere to go because we didn't have living grandparents. They all died before some of us were even born. We were her life; she was not like other parents. Our mother was very strict when we were out of line, but at the same time, she was our best friend. Even when I was young, she told me things that when I think back on them now, I am surprised she did at such a young age. I guess she was preparing me for a future that neither of us could ever have imagined.

So, after the lady in Walmart told me that I needed to get married and have kids, I began to think about my mother's life and how we made her happy. My thoughts were causing me to reflect on some ideas that maybe having a husband and children would make me happy and possibly take away my pain and loneliness.

This was my sophomore year in college and I was still with my first boyfriend at that time, now he was my fiancé because he had proposed on Valentine's Day during my sophomore year in college. However, deep down in my heart I realized I no longer wanted to be with him any longer. But, when he proposed, I couldn't say no; so,I said yes – but inside, I screamed no!

By the end of my sophomore year, I knew that I really needed to be honest with my fiancé and tell him that I could not marry him. I knew that marrying could not bring me the happiness and fulfillment that I was so desperately searching for. Why was I sad if a man could make you happy? I was still miserable and never understood why.

After three years in this relationship, I was tired of feeling guilty. Despite ignoring my personal relationship with God for long, I still knew what I was doing was wrong and that fornication was a sin. When I finally was ready to end it, I couldn't bring myself to do it. He was a sensitive guy and it was clear that he cared a great deal for me. I didn't want to break his heart. It was hard for me to completely end the relationship.

That entire summer, my fiancé was in Rwanda, which made it easier for me because I didn't have to talk to him that much. When my fiancé came back, he came to visit me. By the time he returned, I had made up my mind that I had to end our relationship.

My fiance and I had a talk and I told him that it was not going to work. I made up excuses. I don't even remember exactly what they were. He didn't want to accept the breakup. He told me that my unhappiness was a phase and that it would end. But for me, I was done, I didn't want to be in a relationship with him.

————

Summer ended and I had started my junior year. My fiancé kept calling. I stopped calling him completely because I didn't want to give him false hope. At some point, my fiancé aknowledged that there were differences between us.

To my fiancé , the problem was our religious differences and that had some truth to it. He was a Seventh Day Adventist and I was a born-again Christian. He didn't understand the differences and always said that he didn't see the big deal. My fiancé didn't want to change his religion, and neither did I. Even though I was far from God, I still couldn't see myself going to a different church. I missed the time when God was the center of my life, the way that I had lived my life before I met him. After I met my fiancé, during that wild high school phase; I was living the lifestyle of the average American teenager. I had convinced myself that it was okay to sleep with this man as long I was going to marry him. Still, every time I went to visit him, I felt guilty. Then for a while, I would 'be good' and ask God for forgiveness, but it lasted until I saw him. Then I would be my usual self. When I broke up with my fiancé, I told him all the differences we had between us and the way we wanted to live.

When I told my fiancé that I wanted to change and live a guilt-free life, I was truly convinced. I felt that I was grown and I really wanted to change my life. I started to go to church again on a regular basis and got involved again. This did make me feel better and I felt that I was much happier. I couldn't imagine living with someone who didn't share the same faith.

Throughout my teenage years, I had been battling with issues because I never gave them to God. I was tired of running away from God. I had ignored my sister's pleas for years to turn my life over to God completely. In my sophomore year, long before the engagement, she wrote me a letter when I was still at St. Joseph's. In the letter, she said how she had been watching over me during the years that I spent destroying my life and ignoring God. So, in the end, she had a responsibility as a mother and a sister to speak truth to me. What mortified me the most was when my sister Christina said she knew what me and my fiancé were doing. She told me that my fornication would lead me into more trouble if I didn't stop and surrender my life to God.

After I read that letter, I felt humiliated and didn't even know how I was going to face her. It never crossed my mind that my sister knew what I was doing. I always thought I was clever and was good at hiding it. All these years, I couldn't believe that she knew and never mentioned anything.

When I read the letter, I told my fiancé hat I would never do it again, and I didn't. In fact, I stopped going to visit him because I didn't want to make that mistake again. It was humiliating enough that my sister knew. So, after a whole year of my not seeing him and not being physical with him that's when I realized that we were not meant to be together.

After our relationship ended, I became more serious about life and started thinking about going back to Rwanda. This was summer time of 2003, and I was going to start my junior year in college in the fall. I worked more hours because I wanted to save so I could convince my sister to let me go to Rwanda. I have been thinking about it for quite some time now and I was determined to go at the end of that year during my Christmas break.

Chapter 21

"For I know my transgressions, and my sin is always before me. Against you, you only, have I sinned and done what it is evil in your sight, so that you are proved right when you speak and justified when you judge."

~ Psalms 51:3-4

I have always wanted to return to Rwanda because in my heart I felt that there were unfulfilled mysteries in my mind that needed closure. I wanted to go back to where my parents used to live, and breathe the same air I breathed with them before they were massacred. Surely this was going to make me feel better.

At first, my sister didn't want me to go because she was afraid I would have a nervous breakdown if I went by myself. I told her that I would be fine, because I was more mature now. After she agreed, I bought a ticket to go home for Christmas in the fall of my junior year in college.

Christmas break came, and I was very excited but at the same time I was very nervous. I didn't know what to expect after almost ten years of being away from my country. My memories were nightmares. However, I was determined to go no matter what. When I set my mind to do something, I end up doing it no matter what it costs me.

Christmas break came faster as I expected it would. I had a ticket, but I was unsure of where I was going to stay. There were some people I knew who were still there, but I was not comfortable to live with them after all the years we had been apart. Fortunately, there was a couple from our church fellowship from California who were sent to Rwanda to start a church. My sister told them that I was going to Rwanda. They offered me to stay with them while I was there. I thought that would be a good idea. With them, I would feel more comfortable. Most importantly, they were Christians and we went to the same fellowship.

So, I left the US on a Monday, and that morning it was snowing so badly that all the flights were delayed, By the time I got to Belgium, the flight to Rwanda had already left. There was not another flight until Saturday. The next day, Tuesday morning, my options were to wait a couple of days or take another plane the next day via Uganda. From Uganda, I would have to buy another ticket to take me to Rwanda, since the travel agency I bought the ticket from refused to cover my ticket. I argued with them for a long time and finally gave up and settled for what was possible. The only thing I cared about was getting to Rwanda.

Since we had no other option, we had to stay overnight in Belgium. I am saying "we" because I was with a couple of other students from a school in Pennsylvania. They were going home for vacation. I met them in Chicago, and we all had bought tickets from the same agency. After the flight problem was solved, all of us decided to leave the next day. We had another problem. Since these two students didn't have a visa to visit Belgium, they were not allowed to get out of the Brussels airport. I couldn't believe it. They gave us a little blanket and a little pillow since we would have to spend the night in the airport.

I could have gone outside because I had an American passport, but I didn't think it was fair to my friends. After all, we were suffering together and we were on the same journey. Two of the flight attendants who were there were very nice. They did everything they could do, but there was no end to our problems.

The police was not helpful. They told my fellow travelers to go get visas. My friends waited for hours and hours until finally around 9:00 p.m. they got a twenty-four-hour visa. Meanwhile, while we were fighting for their visas, the flight attendant let me use a phone to call my sister in the US.

As soon as Christina and I were connected, I told her what was happening. She called Pastor Don and Lea, the couple I was going to stay with, to tell them that I was not coming that day.

Finally, when they got their visas, one of the students who had family members living in Belgium, contacted them. They came to get us from the airport. They took us to their house. By the time we arrived it was nearly midnight. We had spent more than twelve hours at that little airport. We slept overnight in Belgium, and the next day, we took a plane to Uganda.

When I got to Uganda it was around eight at night. The plane was about to leave, but the people did not rush us. They waited for us for a couple of minutes to get our luggage. When we went to get our luggage, we couldn't find them. It took me a week to get all mine returned to me. One suitcase ended up in Nairobi. I paid 150 dollars for a one-way ticket to Rwanda from Kampala.

By the time I got to Rwanda that night, it was probably around ten. When I got there, there was nobody there to meet me because they had come the previous day. Nobody expected me to be a day late. Luckily, I was with my traveling companions. Their relatives in Belgium had called their family to tell them that they were coming and what time they would arrive. So, when we got there, their people were waiting for them. Even though my sister in the US knew that I had missed my plane and had informed Pastor Don and Lea that I was not coming, she didn't know that I was arriving the next day because I didn't get a chance to tell her.

However, the family members of one of my new friends let me borrow their cell phone. I had Pastor Don's number in my purse, and thank God for that. My other contacts were in my lost bags. I called them, and since they lived close to the airport it did not take them long to come and get me. That night I was exhausted and I fell asleep as soon as we got to the house.

Chapter 22

"Pay attention and listen to the sayings of the wise; apply your heart to what I teach, for it's pleasing when you keep in your heart and have all of them ready on your lips."

~ *Proverbs 22: 17-18*

The next morning, I didn't realize where I was. I heard the soothing sounds of birds, which I had listened to when I was young, but still, my thoughts were very vague. The birds' sounds of Rwanda are like nowhere else. I can't explain how joyful they sound. You have to wake up in Rwanda to be able to comprehend what I am talking about. When I heard people outside speaking in Kinyarwanda, I became confused. Then I heard someone calling another person from outside. It then became clear to me that I was in Rwanda. I felt a warm feeling inside, and I jumped out of the bed. I didn't want to miss out on anything. I was home!

After I got up, I got to really meet Pastor Don and Lea, since the night before when they came to get me at the airport I was exhausted. I was sleepy and couldn't even remember what they looked like. They were wonderful and pleasant. We had brunch and afterwards the pastor and his wife took me sightseeing.

At first, I felt like a stranger in my own country. Everything looked very odd to me. I felt like a tourist, except a tourist is usually excited to experience a new environment. For me, I felt sad because this was my own country. It was a horrible feeling. When people were staring at me, I felt the same way I felt the first few years when I got to the United States. Now, I was used to it. When people stare, I just ignore it. Yet now I felt like a foreigner in my country. This was still in Kigali. How was I going to feel when I get to my village?

Suddenly I missed my family in the US. It was then I realized that Rwanda was no longer my home. My home was where my family was. Though that feeling didn't last forever. After a few days, I started to remember places and people. The first person I met was Jaxon, Olivia's brother. He was home on vacation. It was nice to see someone familiar.

Then many people came to see me when they heard that I was back in Rwanda. Others called me - the phone was ringing uncontrollably. I couldn't believe how many people found out that I was there. I felt that maybe this trip was not going to end up being bad after all. For the first time after all these years, I saw my two brothers Damascene and Mathias. Mathias was married and had a beautiful little girl and Damascene was still single and looked almost the way I remembered him.

The first week I was in Rwanda I saw Damascene every day because we lived in the same city, but Mathias I saw briefly, a couple of days after I got in Rwanda. He lived in another city, three hours from Kigali and was working every day and he didn't have a day off to come to see me. I have not yet ever seen his wife and daughter so I decided to go visit them.

On my way to visit my brother, I got a chance to visit my friend Liam, Olivia's other brother. Liam has been back in Rwanda for a while because after he graduated from the United States, he returned home. I hadn't seen him for a couple of years. When, I went to see him, I met his uncle Hunter, as well. Liam, Olivia, and Jaxon used to talk about their uncle Hunter, so it was nice to put a face to all the stories they used to tell me of him. We hung out there – the three of us all day and I ended up staying over at Liam's place so we could catch up more.

The next day, I went to visit my brother who lived nearly an hour away from him. I stayed overnight at my brother's house. Then the next day, I left.

On my way back, I passed by Liam's again so we could go back to Kigali together. It was New Year's Eve day and he was going to celebrate the New Year with his family in Kigali. I had told Lea and Pastor Don that I would go and spend New Year's with them.

Liam, however, ended up persuading me to go with him and see his family. He didn't even give me a chance to tell Lea and Don. He drove straight to his parents' home. When we got back to Kigali, it was late and I was sick so I didn't have much energy to fight with him. I had had an allergic reaction to the goat meat we had eaten the night before with Liam and his uncle Hunter. They had taken me to this grill restaurant the night I stayed at his house. Hunter cut the meat that was on a kabob stick Liam ordered for me into little pieces and I thought that it was so sweet and romantic.

The next day I broke into hives all over my body. Liam had to take me to the hospital where I got an injection, but it took me a couple of days to feel better.

The New Year's party held at Liam's parents was nice. Hunter was there as well. It was a big party with food, music and tons of people. Hunter looked so handsome in his suit. I couldn't imagine what I was feeling. After dinner, people danced. A little further into the evening, I began to feel tired, so I sat down with Liam's little sister and cousin.

Out of nowhere, Hunter came and took my hands and asked me to dance. I was so nervous and kept stepping on his toes. He instructed me on how to dance without stepping on him.

After the party was over, I slept there at Liam's parents since it was too late to go back to where I was staying. The next day I told Liam to take me home, but Liam and his mother insisted that I stay because they said I never took a time to visit with them. I didn't know Lea and Pastor Don's number by heart so I could call them. I didn't want them to be worried. Unfortunately, they did become worried and ended up calling my brother. He told them where I was. They proceeded to call. All of this caused me to feel embarrassed and irresponsible.

Later that day, Liam, his girlfriend, Jaxon, Hunter and I went out to Hotel Meridier. I was head over heels in love or should I say in lust with Hunter. I couldn't believe myself. We hung out that day, and then later we went home. It was cold outside so he stood next to me holding me close to him. When we got home, he carried me from the car to the door of Liam's house. This simple romantic jester Hunter did only made what I was feeling inside worse. We were in the living room in the basement where we had been sitting all night. They had a bar there. Hunter, Liam, his girlfriend, and Jaxon sat on stools there drinking, but here I was sitting on Hunter's lap. Don't even ask me how I ended up there.

Eventually, Liam was ready to go to bed, but his girlfriend wanted to go to a club. Liam said he was too tired, but Jaxon and Hunter wanted to go. I didn't want to go either, I was exhausted from the previous night. Liam's girlfriend was whining to him, and Jaxon was getting ready to go out. Hunter and I were left there alone. The next thing I knew we were kissing. To tell the truth, I don't even know what happened. It felt good like it was my first kiss, but at the same time it felt wrong. That minute I knew I was headed for trouble. After they left, I was wondering what the heck was wrong with me.

My thoughts reminded me of how before I left home I had made a commitment to God that I was not going to let anything come between Him and me again. It had been hard to get back into relationship with God again after all those years of disobedience and living how I wanted. After I had rid myself of all those things, I wanted to be better, to let God guide me and Him be the center of my life. But the minute I met this guy, all the commitments to God seemed to come to an end. I couldn't even pray anymore. Hunter was the only thing flooding my mind. After that kiss, the whole night I couldn't sleep. I couldn't wait for the morning to come so I could get away from Hunter. But, at the same time, I wanted to stay close to him. However, my mind was telling me to run. This kiss made me so fearful because they brought feelings I have never experienced in my life. I was filled with mixed emotions; I was so confused and wished I had never done what we had.

The next morning when I got up, I got ready so quickly and told Liam and his mom that I needed to go home. Liam's mom insisted that I needed to have breakfast with them and then the boys would take me. My mind was made up so I persisted that I needed to leave. After trying to convince Liam's mom that I was not hungry, she then insisted that at least I had to wait for the boys to eat. Afterward, Liam's mom suggested that Hunter take me home. As excited as I was inside that he was taking me deep down, I knew this was not a good idea. He dropped me off at Don and Lea's place and promised to call me; though in my mind, I was hoping that he wouldn't call or come to see me again.

When I got to Lea and Don's house, Lea was worried and happy to see me because she knew about my allergic reaction. I didn't even remember that. All that was in my head was the guilt of what I had done, and where my heart was leading.

Sadly, I must admit that the guilt didn't stop me from thinking about Hunter. Actually, I think the more guilt I felt, the more he came to my mind. As pathetic as it may sound, I prayed to God and asked Him to save Hunter. I wanted this man so bad to the point I claimed his soul for God. What was I thinking? Perhaps God would answer my sinful mind's desire?

Moreover, even though Hunter said he was going to call me, he didn't. I didn't call him either. Probably we were both thinking about the same thing. A long-distance relationship was not going to work. Or, he didn't think of me as anything and perhaps some of what happened might have been in my head. I was trying to forget him. I knew I was making a terrible mistake by even thinking about him, even if for a little while.

I only had a week and a half before I was to return to the US, so, it was now time to go visit where my parents used to live. I couldn't have come all this way without going there. Though I knew I could have gone by myself, it was better if I went with someone. I talked to Damascene and my niece Ange and we made plans to go together.

I was wondering how in the world we would get there. Up to that day, there was not vehicle that went there unless you take a private cab, or motorcycle. While I was thinking about how to get to my parents', Liam's mother called me. We talked for a while, and during our talk I told her that I was trying to go to where my parents used to live. She suggested that instead of taking a cab, I should ask Hunter to buy him gas to drive me there. I thought it was a good idea to go with someone I knew instead of taking a cab with someone I didn't know. However, at the same time, I thought that it was dangerous for me to go with him. I didn't know what I might be getting myself into.

Something seemed to take over my thoughts and before I knew it, I was calling people to find out Hunter's number. I asked one of my friends for his number; and she was able to get it from someone else who knew him.

Before I knew it, I called Hunter and I asked him if he could take me up to the area that my parents used to live. He said he would be happy to escort me. Actually, in his words he said that he would do anything for me. We agreed to meet at the bus terminal the next day.

I took a bus by myself without taking my brother or my niece like I was supposed to do. Before we went to my hometown, we stopped at his house to show me where he lived and to say hello to Liam who was at his house. From there we went to my home village. On our way there, we had a flat tire and had to wait for someone to bring us another tire. We waited for an hour or two. His nephew came and brought us a tire. He replaced it and we were able to keep going to my village.

When we got there, I had forgotten how it looked. The whole neighborhood was now deserted. Where there used to be homes, there were overgrown grasses and bushes. I couldn't figure out where our house used to be anymore. When I had come here only one year after the genocide, it had been a bad sight then. At least at that time I could see where the foundation of the house used to be and there had been flowers growing around it. But this time, there was not even a trace of one flower. Hunter and I walked around and looked at things for a while. We sat in overgrown grass for hours, remembering how my father used to work so hard on that land. I was dwelling on how lives that had been destroyed left no traces. The only thing abandoned in that area were a few people left with broken hearts.

My village looked like a ghost town. I couldn't imagine how a town, which was once full of life, could turn into a place that even ghosts didn't want. I looked around thinking about all my uncles and cousins who once lived there and, the good times we had with all the kids while I grew up. They were all gone and forgotten. It was like a bad dream. I couldn't believe that everyone was gone. There was no more listening to my mother's laugh or my father calling my name across from one end of the town; nor the voices of children playing in that neighborhood, all of them had perished without a trace.

———

Hunter was wonderful and took a lot of pictures; although I never saw any of them. I thought about my people, and for the first time, I said goodbye to them. I realized that they were all gone and they would never come back. There had been hundreds of children who had lived there before the genocide. I was the only one who survived from all the people who had been there at the time. For the first time in all those years, I was thankful to God that I now lived in the US and was away from this nightmare. I couldn't imagine how people could live in the very same place where they used to live with their families but now lived with nothing.

My heart went out to the elderly and the single mothers who were left with nothing. They had noone to call on now, when before they had been surrounded by their children and grandchildren; I felt sick to my stomach. I was thankful that I had an older sister. I couldn't imagine what I would have done without her. Would I have been strong enough to take care of my nieces if I had been the one who was left alone with them? I couldn't comprehend how she took care of all of us at such a young age herself, but somehow, she stayed sane. She will always be my role model and my hero. Christina was only 27 years old; she had prematurely become a widow and an orphan. Instead of taking a time to grieve for herself, her family, and her husband, she stood up, dried her tears and took care of her toddler who had just lost a father, her two nieces who lost both parents and her teenager sister. My poor sister had so much on her shoulders and didn't even get a proper chance to grieve. She had to press on and rise to meet the overwhelming, never-before-experienced responsibilities God dropped on her.

After sitting and dreaming, Hunter and I decided that we had endured enough torture and needed to head back. Before we went back to Butare, I had to go and say hello to one of my cousins who was still living nearby. So, we left and went to visit my cousin Alexia, Tim's wife, and her-in-laws. Tim was not there. I was told that he was not getting along with his wife. He was now living with his sister in another region of the country. We sat there for a short time and then we left. We headed back to Butare where Hunter lived. We reached Butare around four in the afternoon.

By the time we got there, I was exhausted from the emotions I felt from being back in my home village. Hunter encouraged me to take a nap for an hour. I didn't think anything of it because I thought it was an innocent suggestion. Besides, I had a lot going on in my mind and couldn't think of anything else. I agreed to take a nap because I was exhausted. That nap ended up being a very bad idea because I ended up staying overnight. The irony was that before I went to Butare from Kigali, I had purposefully not taken anything except the clothes I was wearing, a book to read on the bus and my jacket. I didn't dare take anything else because I wanted to avoid spending the night with him. I didn't want to make that mistake.

I stayed overnight and you can guess the rest. A guy and a girl in the same house both filled with lust. That night was a big mistake. Hunter was now on my mind for sure. I felt filthy and guilty the next day.

———

The following day, I drove with Liam to Kigali from Butare. I was beating myself up – blaming myself for all that had happened. All the way to Kigali. Liam was telling me not to worry about anything and that__ Hunter would never hurt me. I couldn't even listen to what he was saying. My mind was full of guilt, shame, and worries. I was thinking *how could I go from one unsaved man to another and this one I didn't even know?*

Liam dropped me off at that wonderful Christian couple's house. He stayed for a while then went home. I talked to Lea for a while. I wanted to repent and tell her what I did, but I couldn't. I felt humiliated, a failure before God, and I hated myself because of it. This behavior was unacceptable. But I was unable to show all this to Lea, I kept my feeling inside my heart.

I thought to myself, even when I was with my first and only boyfriend I ever had, I never did anything stupid like what Hunter and I had done together – even before I knew him. Then here with this stranger, I let down my guard. The more I thought about it, the more I became disgusted with myself. *Did I have a wild side I didn't know existed?* I knew I was crazy, but not to that point. I always thought I could control myself. Was it because I was so emotional after being at that place? Was I that lonely to end up in the bed of someone I hardly knew? Talking about the guilt I had after that kiss and now this was even more unimaginable. It was a life sentence. I thought I would never be able to live with myself. How was I ever going to face God, now?

For some reason, I thought Lea could tell what was going on in my mind. I probably was being paranoid. I couldn't bring myself to tell her. I had only a few days left before I returned to the US. I knew Lea loved me very much and would have been happy to know what was going on in my mind. She would have prayed for me and given me some advice, but I couldn't bring myself to tell her.

The next day I went to finish getting my hair braided; Before I went to Butare I had it half done. My hair was finished late. When I got home, it was about eight and Lea told me that Hunter called to speak to me. I was happy, but at the same time very sad. I didn't know what to do or say to him. For some reason, I thought about just forgetting about him and just taking what I did as a one-time mistake and move on.

Even if I was thinking that way, I don't ever think I asked God to forgive me. How could I repent when my heart was filled with sin? I just felt numb and stupid. In my heart, I felt that God would never forgive me.

I called Hunter back, and we talked about nothing. After that, I think we talked a few more times over the phone. I didn't have that much time left in Kigali. He promised that we would see each other again before I went back to the US. He kept his promise.

The day I went back to the US, he got up at five in the morning and drove to Kigali to see me. Since I couldn't tell Lea the truth about where I was going, I told her that I had more gifts that I needed to buy for people. More sin was covered by another sin. I went to meet him that morning around eight and we spent the whole day together. My flight was around seven and I got back home around four. They all ready to take me to the airport and Hunter was there until I left. We promised each other to keep in touch. My flight back to the US seemed short. I spent most it sleeping and dreaming about Hunter.

When I arrived back in the US, everyone was so excited to see me. Everyone wanted to hear about my trip. I didn't want to face them. What will I tell them? I left as a Christian on fire, so I had to go to church on Sunday. After that Sunday, I don't think I went back again. The guilt was drowning me, and for several days I wanted to write to Lea to tell her what I had done in Rwanda because I felt that I betrayed her trust in me. Still, I couldn't go back to church, and I couldn't even repent because I was thinking about Hunter all the time. Besides, before God could forgive me, I had to forgive myself, which I couldn't. Instead of forgiving myself and asking God to forgive me, I had the urge to bring Hunter here to the US. I thought maybe by bringing him to the US, I could make my sin go away.

I thought that if he became my husband, the sin I committed would not look as bad as it was. All of this was going through my head, though I never mentioned any of it to him or anyone else. So, after I left Rwanda, Hunter and I really did keep in touch through email and phone calls. My phone bills were never under $300 each month despite the international calling cards. Each month, I was paying large fees for over my allotted minutes. He sent me nice emails, but because it was more expensive for him to call me, I told him that I would always call him. From January through March, there was so much love between us. At least that's how it felt for me.

Then something happened. I still don't know what happened exactly, but he stopped our communication. I sent him an email, and I called him. He never returned any of my messages. I don't know if he was attempting to get rid of me or not. It is still a mystery to me. Since I am very stubborn and persuasive when it comes to what I want, I couldn't let him win. I kept calling and sending him emails. All this didn't work because he was more stubborn than I /was becoming obsessed with him, and knew I needed to stop. For some reason, thoughts of Hunter kept filling my mind. For few months, we didn't talk at all. I think three to four months went by without us talking. From time to time, I thought about him and I told myself that I had to snap out of it and forget about the guy. So, I gave up, and full of shame, I knew now that I had lost a boyfriend. One night, I decided to bow down and ask God to forgive me for my relationship with my new attachment. I felt that what I did was wrong, and what I was planning to do was even worse than that. It's pathetic how I thought I could control my life and cover my sins with other sins, and then when that didn't work out as I thought; my next move was to take God as my last resolution.

The thought of trying to manipulate Hunter to come to the US and possibly marry me to cover my wrongdoing was horrible. I thought maybe this happened for a reason. I made peace with God and myself and let the thoughts go. God showed me that I was nothing without Him. When I think about it; it was pathetic and embarrassing how I always turned to God when there was no man around.

Eventually, I decided to focus on my schoolwork and forget about Hunter. Everything was going well, I had forgotten about him and had even buried what we had done together. I decided that it was part of my past, and I needed to move on, to take it as one of life's lessons.

Then one day I was taking a nap after school, and I dreamed about him. When I woke up, I felt so sad. I missed Hunter very much. I said to myself that maybe it was not lust; *yeah, sure!* Maybe I really loved him. I picked up the phone and I called him. To my surprise, he picked up. It was so nice to hear his voice. His voice was one of the things that I loved most about Hunter. So, we talked. After fifteen minutes, I hung up. I felt such relief. After a couple of weeks, I called him again. We talked, and he told me that he would send me an email, which he did.

From then on, we talked, and corresponded with each other. Things got back to the way they were before as though nothing had

153

happened. After four months of talking, we felt that we really needed to be near each other. I decided to bring him to the US. We talked about it, and we both got excited about the idea of him coming. I applied for Hunter to move to the US. We were so excited; I couldn't wait to see him again after all this time.

The national visa center processed his paperwork, and sent it to the American Embassy in Nairobi, Kenya. It was so much work, but I knew when everything was done, it would all be worth it. We went through a rough time for him to get to the US. He went to Nairobi three times for the interview. After a lot of sleepless nights, headaches, and several phone calls between the US, Nairobi, and Rwanda, he finally got his paperwork. We applied in the US in November of 2004 but it wasn't approved until the end of April or beginning of May of 2005. He finally got to the US on June 6, 2005. It took a month for him to get ready to come.. I was so happy and couldn't wait to see him. I went to the airport with a friend to pick him up. I couldn't believe he was finally here with me. When we got together, the period of silence was never mentioned and I didn't even ask him about it. The fear of losing him was greater than my curiosity to learn the real reason he had cut off communication for that short period of time.

Chapter 23

"Delight yourself in the Lord and he will give you the desire of your heart."

~Psalms 37:4

Before Hunter came, I had one major problem to solve: finding him a place to stay. I was back in the church and happy. That's the lie I told myself anyway. When we started talking again, I continued going to church. I thought to myself that even if he came to the US, I could find a place for him to stay. I was thinking of maybe asking some of my good male friends who lived in Boston to put him up, but I felt that if I put Hunter somewhere other than with me, it would be like abandoning him. I didn't want him to feel that way after all this time we had waited to see each other.

Another problem that I faced was because Hunter was coming on a fiancé visa, we had 90 days to get married or he had to return to Rwanda. I was nervous because I didn't want to marry him that soon. Besides we really didn't know each other well enough to get married. Because of all this, a lot was going on in my mind. I couldn't focus anymore or go to church and feel good. My sister kept telling me that I should go talk to my pastor. I didn't want to tell him about my relationship with Hunter and besides, I was so ashamed of my lifestyle, too. I knew better, even if I didn't want to face the reality. From what I knew, getting involved with an unsaved man always ended badly.

Eventually, I ended up talking to my pastor. Pastor Laine told me that it was not a good idea to bring Hunter to the US right now since we didn't know each other that well and Hunter was not a Christian. I don't think Hunter even went to church at that time.

I thought carefully about all of this, but I felt it was too late to call the embassy to tell them to stop the process of his paperwork. Besides, I didn't think it was fair to Hunter to change my mind after I got him excited. I didn't have the nerve to tell him that I wasn't going to go through with it. Besides, who was I to judge him? In fact, there were times when I felt I was worse than him. I never showed any signs of Christianity. Even if I had all these battles in my mind, I never told him.

I will never forget what my pastor asked me. I wish I knew what he had meant. As a guy and a man of God, he knew what he was talking about. I didn't get it that time. He asked me if Hunter had asked me to marry him. I told him that he hadn't, but we had talked about getting married someday. The pastor said, he couldn't marry us if we went through with the marriage. He believed what I was doing was not right. Deep down inside, I knew he was right. Though I followed my own desires instead of what my heart was telling me. I continued following up the process of getting Hunter's papers. I didn't listen to my pastor. I kept going through with the process of bringing Hunter to the US. Looking back, I wish I had listened to Pastor Laine. Someday, I want to apologize to my pastor, but I am sure he knows that in my heart I regretted it more than anything.

Even if I was very delighted when he got his papers to come to the US, at the same time because of what was happening I didn't know what I was going to do with him when he got to the US. I knew that for sure it was not right to put him in my apartment. So, before he came, I talked to my sister, I asked her if I could go back home and Hunter could have my apartment. I asked my roommate, she told me that it was okay, that he could stay. I also told her if she wanted to, she could come with me to stay at my sister's house. We were like sisters, and my family loved her.

Genie insisted that she would be fine living in the apartment with Hunter. My sister laid down the rules. She said that if I lived with her, I had to promise that I would not sneak around behind her back. I also had to promise not to do anything inappropriate with Hunter, because that would be hypocritical and sinful. To tell you the truth, when I promised her that I would not do anything God wouldn't approve of - with him I was being truthful. In my heart, I believed that I could control myself. After all that time being away from him, I believed I could abstain. Besides, at least Hunter was here where I could talk to him and see him whenever I wanted.

One thing that stayed on my mind was - I wanted to make up to God for what I had done when I was in Rwanda. I also wanted to set the right example for my nieces who looked up to me, and redeem my years of rebellion. That's what I told myself anyway.

Hunter arrived on Wednesday during our mid-week service. I took him home. No one was there except us. All those promises I made to my sister didn't last for even an hour. By the time my sister and my nieces came to my house to meet Hunter, we had already done everything and were now trying to appear innocent.

They talked to him for a while. However, because it was a school night they had to leave, my sister asked me if I was coming home with them. That night, I made up some excuse about not going home with them. I couldn't tell her the truth about what I had done. But I knew if I went with her, I would be lying to her. Before she left, she warned me that I was heading for trouble. I told her not to worry and that I would be fine, but I wasn't.

From that point forward, Hunter and I lived together. I ended up not ever going to my sister's house at all. The first week he was there I went to church. Can you imagine how I was feeling inside? I felt like a devil sitting in the church. After that Sunday, I never attended church there again.

After that all I did was work and be with Hunter. During the first few weeks, there was nothing else that mattered in my life except him. I didn't even go to see my family as often as I had before his arrival. In the past I didn't let two days go by without seeing or talking to them. I should have known that I was heading for trouble. When I asked Hunter to go with me to visit them, he never wanted to go (even for me). Sometimes I begged him to come when they invited us over, but he never wanted to go. He seemed like he was not interested in getting to know them. Though he didn't say it aloud, it was obvious. It made me sad, because I always told my family that I would never marry someone who would not love them. They are the only family I have, and I couldn't imagine being with someone who would say that he loved me but didn't care about my family. Even if it bothered me a lot, I wanted everyone to get along.

My sister tried to get to know him, but Hunter, never really made an effort. After a while, I thought maybe I should give him time. Hopefully, he would come around. It surprised me because I had never met anyone who didn't like my family. Everyone I brought home loved them. Several of my friends today still call my sister and go visit her and my nieces even though I don't live there anymore. I was hurt and sad when Hunter showed me that he was not interested in knowing them. I could care less if everyone else hated them, but not Hunter. He was the most important person in my life. Once I asked him why was he being that way. Then, he told me that it was very hard to trust or open up to people he didn't know. He asked me to give him time. I believed him because I know we are all different. I needed to accept who he was if I wanted him in my life.

The first month was happy, but at the same time it was hard. My sister was always telling me that it was not right to live with a man I was not married to. I knew she was right. She was always telling me that we had to do the right thing. I didn't know what to do. I didn't feel that we were ready for marriage when we didn't know each other that well. We lived in sin, and most of the time I was living in guilt. But for some reason, when you sin so much, there is a voice that keeps telling you it is all right. After a while, you make peace with it. Even if I knew that it wasn't right, I was happy when I was with him. When I was alone, I was miserable. My sister came to talk to us about living together. I don't remember what Hunter told her, but I guess he said that he would give her an answer soon. I kept my mouth shut because I knew better. I understood being her little sister she has a right to look after me and correct me when I was wrong. Every day she would say, "Anamaliya, what if this guy is using you?" I argued that he wasn't, but deep down I knew this was a possibility. Besides, I brought all this to myself and I had to face the consequence. However, since we had to get married in ninety days, I didn't think we had an option anyway. We had to get married in the ninety-day period, or he had to go back home.

Even though there was a lot going on when we were living together. I felt that all we needed was time and things would get better. The month of June went by fast because I was busy and distracted. I didn't want to marry him before the end of the ninety days. At least those three months would give us both a little time to get to know each other.

Eventually, however, I came to the realization that we had to get married soon because he was getting bored sitting home and doing nothing all day. Every time I came home from work I found him sitting on the couch. I felt so bad since he couldn't work until we got married. In the meantime, we found out that he could apply for working papers before he got his residency. I was glad because, if he got his working papers, at least he would have something to do besides sit at home. Then, we could get married later when his visa was about to expire. But when we got there, they informed us that those papers would be valid until the expiration of his visa. We felt it was useless to pay two hundred dollars for just a couple of months and then pay more when we applied for his permanent residence.

We decided to get married because when we applied for his residency, Hunter would get papers which would allow him to work for up to one year. Since we didn't have many options, on July fifth, 2005 we went to the city hall and got married. After a few days, we applied for all the papers he needed. The working papers arrived in a month. I was so happy when he got them. Now he would be busy, and working would take his mind off of waiting for his other green card to come.

When we decided to get married, we said we were not going to tell anyone. However, the night before, I met my sister at a birthday party. I felt that I couldn't marry without telling her. Guilt came over me. I remember how she used to tell me that she would buy me a beautiful wedding gown when I got married. I thought about how I had never even given her that chance. The least I could do was to tell her the truth about what Hunter and I were planning to do. I told her. She felt that it was good for us to get married. Being naïve, I didn't think Hunter would mind if I told my sister. When I got home, I told him that I had told my sister. He said that it was okay, but I could tell that he wasn't comfortable with it. The next day I called city hall, and they said we didn't need to bring anyone else besides us. So, we went alone. I was so nervous though thinking that I was probably making the biggest mistake of my life. I began to wonder whether it was a good idea to marry this man. However, I felt stuck. I went ahead and signed my life away. We signed all papers we needed and then they gave us our marriage certificate.

Afterwards, we went out to eat and then we went home. We then went on with our lives, but from time to time I asked myself whether I had made a mistake. It was too late to change anything now. I just hoped things would work for us. He told me that someday we would go back to Rwanda and have a real wedding.

However, during those months that Hunter was sitting home waiting his paper to come. He became very reserved. He would remain silent for an entire week. I would get worried sometimes, but at the same time, I understood him. I couldn't imagine sitting home for weeks doing nothing, especially for a guy. I knew if it was me I would go crazy too. Even though he had access to my car, there was not much to do in

Dover, New Hampshire. By the end of his two weeks in Dover, he was done exploring. After that, he just sat home and watched TV. When he was down, I would try to talk to him, but he would blow me off. I learned to leave him alone and wait until he snapped out of it. I never knew if he would get up happy or sad. He was so unpredictable.

Every time I tried to see if there was anything I could do for him, he would blow me off. He said he didn't like to talk or share his issues. He said, "I never had anyone asking me what was wrong with me even when I was a kid. What makes you so sure that you would suddenly change me and I would tell you my problems?" It made me sad to have him refuse to acknowledge me when I asked him what was wrong. It was just that I cared about him and didn't want him to feel that he was alone.

Sometimes, it got to the point that it made me so mad. I said "Could you imagine living with someone so unpredictable, someone lying next to you who was like a rock." He would respond by saying if he was so hard to live with, then maybe he should leave. All this was hard for me too. I was learning to live with someone. I never had so much responsibility in my life. I learned to sacrifice and be patient. He never got the point. I was the only one who seemed to care about our relationship. One day I got so angry and I told him that I didn't see why we should waste our time living together and suffering through it when clearly our relationship was going nowhere. He told me that I should give it time because the problems we were having were normal for every couple.

It was very difficult to get to know him, if he told me something once, and maybe I didn't pay attention because I thought he was not being serious, he would later use it against me. This was mainly because he always said things laughing, or as though he was making a suggestion. I never knew when he was serious. Then later I would pay the price. Many times, I had no idea what our disagreements were all about. He was quick to tell me if he thought I looked terrible, but never mention if I looked good.

Come to think of it, I don't know if he ever told me that I looked good in the few months that we lived together. He never told me that I was beautiful. Like every woman I needed to hear from my man that he thought I was special. Every woman wants her man to show her that he is attracted to her and cares about her. All I got from Hunter was criticism, not one compliment. I just learned to know that I looked good if he didn't make a negative comment. When I expressed to him how I felt, he admitted that he had that problem. He said he was willing to change, but he didn't. I guess when you have a habit; it takes a long time to change. When we talked, we were good for a while. Then other things will come up so it was an unending battle.

Chapter 24

"Many are the plans in a person's heart, but it is the Lord's purpose that prevails."

Proverbs 19:21

I came to accept this guy as mine and took him as he was. I knew that I, too, was far from perfect, but by compromising, Hunter and I could build a life together. Besides, putting two total different people under the same roof, and expecting everything to be perfect is unrealistic. It took a while to adjust to that change. Since we both were genocide survivors and had lost our families, I felt that we were more connected and had more in common than just our love for each other. He used to tell me that if for some reason he died, his family would have no men left in their family because all of his brothers had been killed. All he had left were his sisters. So, I felt that someday Hunter and I would have children and create a family of our own; that way each of us wouldn't feel lonely or out of place. I thought children would bring blessings to us both.

———

The end of July of that year was my birthday. My sister Christina planned a surprise birthday party for me. Later, I learned that she had called Hunter and told him that she wanted to plan a birthday party. However, she wanted to make sure he didn't mind. Nobody told me anything about the plans, of course, but when someone asked me where my party was going to be and what I wanted for my birthday, I could only answer one of their questions. Then I knew there was something happening that was not being discussed with me. My sister had invited a few friends and others from my church. The party was at the home of a family friend from my church. When I got there, I saw many people I wasn't expecting. There was food and gifts some were addressed to both Hunter and I. Getting gifts that had both of our names on them seemed odd since Hunter didn't have a birthday in July, but I didn't think much of it.

When the time came to cut the cake, my sister announced something for which I was not prepared. She told them that the reason she threw the party was to celebrate my birthday and to introduce Hunter as my husband, to our friends. I wasn't ready for all those speeches, and I had no idea that Christina was going to make an announcement about us.

Eventually, I found out that Hunter was not happy about my sister telling our life plans. Personally, I did not see the big deal of Christina's announcement, I was actually glad that the secret was out. I thought that was so thoughtful and sweet of my sister to throw a party for us. I wanted my friends to know Hunter. I really didn't see the point of hiding anyway. Hiding our marriage status was bizarre, but that man had me under his thumb, anything he said I followed without thinking twice of it or questioning him at all.

Later, I don't know what happened, but Hunter and I stopped talking for a couple of days like we always did. We had so many of these little days, they came to be part of our relationship. Then later in the week, Hunter and I went out with our friends in Boston. He had a lot to drink and he was in a good mood. I briefly forgot all the drama we had been through over the last couple of days. That's what dancing did to me, I guess, since I don't drink. We were standing alone, and then I got close to him. I gave him a hug and when I went to embrace him, he held me back. I asked Hunter why was he pushing me away and why had he shut me down over the past few days. Hunter told me that my sister should not have done what she did; and I shouldn't have told her our business since we agreed we were not going to tell anyone. Hunter said that it showed that I didn't trust him. If I did, I would have kept our business private and trusted him completely without involving other people. He went on to tell me everything I did was wrong. Some of what he said was true, and I had to admit it and so, I apologized. I told him that I didn't know my sister was going to make that announcement. I don't know why I couldn't find words to defend myself as he attacked my character, I always found myself listening, nodding to him and absorbing all negativity he said about me. Afterward, I would meditate on his attacks toward me and my lifestyle. At some point, I told Hunter that I didn't think he showed that he cared much about me. He said if he hadn't loved me, he would not have moved to the US for me. I really believed him. Even though we were struggling, I convinced myself that it was not that bad. I thought we were just like any other couple trying to fit in each other's lives and trying to learn more about each other. Really, at the time, I loved this man to death, and I wanted everything to work out for us. However, most of the time, I felt that I was the only person trying so hard to make it work in this relationship instead of us being together as a couple.

Then in September of 2006, I found out that I was pregnant. I was not ready for this child. Both of us were unprepared. First, I had not finished school yet; I had one class to finish before I would be able to receive my bachelor's degree. Plus, I always hoped that I could go to graduate school to become a counselor. Plus, Hunter didn't have his papers yet and I was working two jobs to make ends meet. During that time, I took three pregnancy tests. They all were positive, and I was horrified. I thought it would be too much for Hunter to handle so I hid the news from him for a couple of days.

Living through all this made me wonder why women in struggling relationships always do what a man wants? My experience taught me men always accuse women of getting pregnant on purpose. What kind of women would want to get pregnant by uncaring/untruthful men on purpose? Who are we protecting by hiding their abuse from them? We are the one who is carrying the biggest burden. I should not have hidden the pregnancy from him, much less my feelings about him and being pregnant, period. Nevertheless, I could not hide it any longer because I felt that he had a right to know. One night when we were lying in bed, I told Hunter that I thought I was pregnant. He got quiet.

I asked, "No comment?"

Hunter responded, "What do you want me to say?"

"At least please tell me something and tell me how you feel about it," I pleaded.

He asked, "How do you know that you are pregnant anyway?"

I told him about the pregnancy tests and admitted I could also feel it somehow. He told me to go to bed, and we would talk about it the next day. The next morning, Hunter took me to work. Neither of us said anything on the way there. Halfway to work, he eventually turned to me and said, "You know what, a child is not a bad thing and besides I am not getting any younger. It is just the situation we are in and that is not ideal."

I understood completely and was relieved that he was okay with it. Then when we were nearly at work, all of sudden he said, "You are not the first one you know."

Shocked and caught by a surprise, I asked, "What are you talking about? Do you have another child I don't know about?" I asked.

"I might!" Hunter responded.

Of course, I was confused. I could not believe my ears being that I had been with him for two years. We talked every day, I knew his family, and I never knew that he had had a child. How could he hide this from me?

His response was, "We didn't have time to talk about it, like we never planned to have this baby," he said.

I couldn't believe my ears. However, Hunter never did clarify it and we did not talk about the other woman either. I did not know for sure if he had a child. He just led me in this stupid conversation, which did not make sense to me until I got to work. I didn't even understand what his point was in telling me something like this when I had just told him I was carrying his child. In the moment, I was trying so hard to keep it together and not scream or cry. I felt a lump growing in my throat and tightness in my chest. When I got to work, I got out of the car – feeling ill and couldn't breathe, I felt that I would not be able to do my job as an optician's assistant, much less go to school (which I was still doing at the time). After a few hours, I told the lady I was working with that I didn't feel well and needed to go home. I called my other job and told them I was not coming in because I was sick. Afterward, I called my roommate, and she came to pick me up. I went home feeling sick to my stomach. Hunter was sitting on the couch when I got home. I didn't speak to him, and he didn't bother to say anything to me either. I went straight to bed.

Hunter never wanted to take the initiative to talk to me, even when it was his fault. He could go for days without talking until I got sick of silence and had to ask him what was wrong. That night I asked him if he took pleasure in hurting me. He told me it was not his intention to hurt me. It is that, when he was mad he said things he didn't even know where they were going to come from. I asked him if he really had a kid. He told me he didn't and apologized for making me mad and confusing me. I still don't know if he really doesn't or he told me he didn't to shut me up. He had a way of charming me. I was so in love with him I never saw through his manipulations.

For a few days after that, things were good. I even thought Hunter seemed excited about the baby because he told me that it made him feel like he was not alone anymore now that he had a child on the way. It didn't take much to make me happy. He cooked for me and told me that I needed to eat so I would not starve his baby. It made me so happy to think that I was carrying a child we created together inside of me.

However, the happiness didn't last for long. A week later, he fell back into his mood again. He wouldn't talk to me, and this time, I didn't know what to do. He was like this for a week. I tried to talk to him but to no avail. I was pregnant for the first time and I was so scared and didn't have anyone to comfort me either. I did everything I could to get him out of his mood. I tried to leave him alone. At that point, I didn't know what to do anymore. I decided to write him an email. I told him that I understood how he was feeling, and I knew that it was hard to be thinking that Hunter was going to have a child when he didn't even have anything or anybody else in this country. I told him that it was as hard for him as it was for me. I suggested he try to see how we could go through the pregnancy together. After pouring out my heart to him via email, I sent it to him that night and went to bed. He didn't get the email until the next day when I was at work.

When Hunter came to pick me up from work that night, I noticed that he was in a better mood. We talked all the way home. When we got home, he opened up and told me that he couldn't believe that he had a child on the way when he didn't have a way to support that child. I told him that I understood completely, but ignoring me or being depressed would not change the fact that the baby was on the way. We talked about it, and then he told me that the email I had sent helped him a lot.

Finally, Hunter was opening up to me, which of course made me glad. He became himself again for a short time. Then, after several days, we were lying in bed and he said a lot of mean things to me. He always had a way of putting me down, and it broke my heart to see that he didn't have respect for me. What made me even madder was when Hunter talked about how, "we wanted to make him my husband" since the first time he came to the US. The "we," was my sister and I. I couldn't believe it. How could you make a thirty-one-year old man into your husband if he didn't want to be? How was I trying to make him my husband? I admitted I loved him, but I was not desperate to make anyone my husband who didn't have any desire to be.

After that night, I tried to ignore all the hurt I felt. Hunter was in a better mood for a while, and then he became his usual moody self again. I could never guess what mood this man would be in when he got up. He was depressed for another three weeks. Hunter didn't even want to take me to work anymore. He just sat at home without getting out of the house. I tried to talk to him like before, but this time it was like talking to a brick wall. I tried reaching him through emails like before, but that didn't work, either – I just gave up. Can you imagine sleeping next to someone who doesn't talk to you for days?

By the end of October, I had had it. I was an emotional wreck myself because of the changes taking place in my body. Also, I had to deal with this guy who didn't even care how I felt. The baby was never mentioned. He never asked me how I was feeling. It was as though the child I was pregnant with no longer existed. My hormones were raging, and I could feel it all in my body. I was exhausted from working two jobs. All I had to come home to was a mute man.

One night I felt so alone and missed Hunter so much. So, I went to bed, but I couldn't sleep. I went to him and told him that I really missed him and wanted him to be himself again. Hunter told me that there was nothing he could do about that. Then, he told me to go to bed before he said something hurtful to me. *What kind of threat was that, I thought to myself?* I continued to press him. I said, "Hunter, let's talk." Hunter said we have a lot to talk about and that there is nowhere to begin. Then Hunter said if I wanted to talk, I should ask him some questions and he would answer them.

I proceeded to ask, "Are you mad because I am pregnant?"

Hunter said that it was a mistake for him to have come to the US. And he wished he hadn't done it. I told him that it was not a mistake that he came. The mistake was us living together right away without getting to know each other first. "Why don't you go and get an abortion and things could go back to normal as it was before you were pregnant?" Hunter asked.

I couldn't believe my ears. How could I abort a child made with someone I was in love with, and who was supposed to be my husband? I told him that I was unable to get an abortion. Even in the midst of being deeply sunk into sin, I still had the fear of God in me. Just the thought of Hunter mentioning it astonished me. Here he was – the guy I loved and was looking forward to spending the rest of my life with – and he was telling me to abort a child we created together. Despite the circumstances, I wanted this child. I told him that abortion was not an option. Genocide had wiped out most of my family; there was no way I was going to abort this little gift God have given me regardless of my sinful life.

He responded by saying, "Do you know how many girls killed my children?"

Then I understood what he meant when he told me that I was not the first. I couldn't believe this man! I told him that I was not those girls, and I would never wish to be like them. Besides, "Do you think those girls are happy for what they have done?" I asked. He told me *probably not*. I told him that I was not going to be like those other women, and whether he decided to be in this child's life or not, the baby would always be there and we would be fine. I told him that I would be happy to raise my child alone. I said this without realizing that this would one day be my fate.

Hunter went on telling me hateful things. For the first time I saw that I was living with a heartless man. I asked him if he had ever loved me. After Hunter replied that I wished I never had asked him. He said, "I never loved you, and since the day I came here, I've tried to love you and tried to change you. If you hadn't gotten pregnant I would still have been trying to love you. And besides, what made you think that I loved you? Have I ever given you anything to show you that I loved you? Have I ever even bought you flowers? Besides making love with you, which meant nothing. It was like having sex with any of the other girls I used to sleep with, what else did we do special like other people who love each other? Did I ever tell you that I loved you? And If I did, it was because you said it first and I didn't want to hurt your feelings."

After he told me all this, I wished I had never opened my mouth. Up to this day, I don't know why he told me all these hateful things. Did he want to hurt me? I always wondered if this was the strategy he used to anger his previous girlfriends so they would go and get abortions. This is still a mystery to me. I couldn't imagine how a normal person could tell you something like that, even if they were your enemy. I know there are things we think in our heads, but we never say them out loud. He tried to convince me to get an abortion so that everything would get back to normal. But after I heard him speak, I was not sure if I would ever feel normal around him. I felt used. Hunter made me feel like a cheap whore. I felt sick and felt like I had been making love to a stranger in my own bed. At that moment, I just wanted to crawl in a hole and die. I couldn't believe what was happening to me. This was not a horror movie or bad dream - it was my life, my reality.

I couldn't believe I was carrying the child of someone like that. Later he told me that the child I was carrying would be no different from him. I refused to believe that, because I knew that this child had half of my genes. No matter how we felt or how this child was created, my child belonged to God. I didn't know why God was giving me this precious gift that I didn't deserve. But, I knew in my heart, I had to protect my child. I knew in my heart and by the promise of God my child will never be like his father. In my heart, I felt that my child was mine and was a gift from God. No one was going to take that away from me. I decided to not let the stress of this relationship cause me to lose my baby or to have a traumatized child.

That same night, as I was sitting there, I couldn't cry. I was numb. All of a sudden, I heard a knock on the door, and without thinking, I got up and went to open it. My whole family was standing at the door holding a cake for me, my three nieces, Aurore, Carine and Gabriella and my sister Christina. It was not a time to celebrate, but I couldn't have been happier to see my family. I don't know what came over me, but I burst out and cried before I even said hello to them. They didn't know whether to come in or stay out. They came in. I sat in the hallway, and my niece Aurore, who is so emotional, sat next to me and cried as well, without even knowing why I was crying. My family showed up when I needed them the most. Call it chance - either way, I call it my God being intentional. I felt it was God's way of telling me that *He's got my back* and He loves me regardless of my sins and my sinking sand situation, which I got myself into.

My sister and my two nieces came in next and said hello to Hunter. He sat there talking to them like nothing had happened. They didn't stay for long probably because they were not comfortable, and I couldn't tell them what was happening. They went home, but I could only imagine what they were thinking on their way there. At that moment I wanted so badly to go home with them, but I felt that this was my battle to fight. I was not a little girl, anymore. I knew that I had a family that loved me so much, and friends who I could count on if I needed anything. I knew that I could live without Hunter. If he was going to continue to mistreat me I was better off living without him.

After my sister and my nieces left my house confused, my sister called to ask me what was wrong. I could not tell her the whole story over the phone, I told her I would tell her later. I got up and went to bed.

The next day I didn't want him to know how weak I felt, I got up and went to work. I wanted something to get my mind off of him. I didn't want him to break me. I tried not to let the situation I was, in affect, my work. I had been through worse in my life. After all this, I looked at him as someone else. I couldn't sleep next to him anymore. I just felt sick.

I moved to my roommate's room. However, her mattress was on the floor, after a week of sleeping on her bed, I had a major backache and I couldn't sleep there. I couldn't bear the pain anymore. I had to go back to my bed, but really didn't want to sleep next to Hunter anymore. I thought about going to my sister's house, but I felt that since I was paying for my own apartment, I shouldn't live somewhere else. I wanted to kick him out, but being the person, I am, I didn't have the strength to ask him to leave. I worried about where he would go if I made him leave. After all, I was the one who brought him to the US. In my heart, I felt that I was responsible for him regardless of how he was treating me.

In the meantime, while all this happened, he had gotten his work authorization documents and a friend from my church had hired him. When he started working, I was happy because I thought maybe all the stress and anxiety of having a baby and silence would go away. Instead, things got worse.

Our relationship was never the same after that conversation we had. Every time I entered the house, I replayed our conversation in my head over and over again. After a while, I felt that he had to go, or I needed to get out.

My sister told me that before he left she needed to talk to him. I asked her not to mention me because you can't force someone to love you or stay with you if they don't want to. She said, "Don't worry, that's not the reason I am going to talk to him. Even if he's not looking for a counsel, I think someone should talk to him before he leaves. I feel like I have a responsibility as your elder to tell you the truth, I don't think much of the guy, but I will give him a chance and hear him out." So, she talked to Hunter but she didn't tell me what they talked about. The only thing she said was to "Just forget about that man and go on with your life because he used you. He has no respect for you."

I wanted Hunter to leave, but I didn't see where he was going to go. He did not have his official residency paperwork despite being authorized to work in the US. He didn't even have his driver's' license yet. My sister got mad one day and told me that she didn't see why I

173

was being stubborn and nice to this man who didn't care about me at all. Unfortunately, none of what she said changed my mind. I wasn't yet ready to let him go.

In late October, my sister and I were at a church party, and I asked Christina what her and Hunter had talked about. I wanted to know because after they had a talk, my sister really didn't think highly of him and that's was unlike her. Christina said I really didn't want to know, but after I kept bugging her; she told me. He had told her, that he couldn't believe that she announced our marriage in front of all those people. Hunter admitted to my sister that he thought it was inappropriate because there was no marriage at all. He said that when he met me in Rwanda I told him that if he ever needed any papers to come to the US that I would be happy to assist him. He was actually surprised when he came here and I put him in the same house as myself. The fact that we slept together didn't mean anything to him because when I was in Rwanda we slept together. He also said that he didn't even know that I had a family, who cared that much about my morals because when he saw me he thought I was too independent. He also told her that when he came to the US he had enough money to afford rent for himself for three months.

After my sister told me this I was livid, I couldn't believe that he had the nerve to tell my sister all this. He knew my sister was like a mother to me. She raised me, and I respected her. He violated our relationship and any trust I had left for him. He left nothing on the table: the nights in Rwanda. I was also shocked to learn he had come with money - something he never mentioned while I was pregnant and working two jobs to pay bills. All this showed me was that he had no respect for my family, or me. After my sister told me all of this, I just sat there. I couldn't even talk. I was ashamed and humiliated. My sister assured me that I didn't have to feel embarrassed because she knew everything before he even mentioned it to her. She also said that she saw the way I acted when I came back from Rwanda, calling him and desperate to bring him to the US.

Calmly, Christina said to me, "You didn't have to spell it out for me. To me, what Hunter told me didn't make you look bad, it made me think less of him. He just has no respect for you. You have to let go of your feelings and let him go."

I sat there numb. I felt that I had to get out there. I left the party without saying bye to anyone. I rushed back home, I had never been angrier in my life. When I got home, he was sitting on the couch. For the first time in my life I wished I had the courage to scream at Hunter and tell him to just *go* because he had already caused me enough pain. I couldn't bear to look at him anymore. But, I am not that kind of person. With God's grace, I calmed down, went in the room and got on computer literally did nothing on it; I was using it to distract myself as I waited for the right moment to talk to him, because the computer was right across from him.

I acted as though I didn't know he had talked to my sister. "How come you never told me that you talked to Christina?" I asked him.

"Aren't you the one who sent her?" Hunter said. Hunter always had a way of twisting things around. I told him that I didn't send her. I really didn't care whether he believed me or not.

Then I asked Hunter, "Was it really necessary to tell her all those things you said to her?"

He responded, "Didn't I tell her the truth? Isn't that what you always wanted?"

"Since when did you start telling the truth?" I asked him.

Hunter replied, "How come you care about when you tell the truth, and then when it comes to other people you expect them to lie for you?"

Then I said, "Hunter I really never wanted you to lie but there are things you just don't say. What I did in Rwanda is not something I am proud of and I am sure I would regret it for the rest of my life. You had no reason to really tell my sister all you said. I am so sorry I slept with a dog." I just didn't even know where that word out of my mouth came from, but, the minute I let it out, I wished I could take it back. It was too late. Hunter got so furious I thought he was going to kill me. He responded by calling me some names I don't remember. He got up and went outside probably to calm himself down. I am very sure if we had been in Rwanda, things could have gotten worse. He might have slapped me or something. This was it for us. I told Hunter that I needed him to leave. Then he told me that he was planning to leave the next day anyway. There was so much pain and so much damage that will not really be repaired.

I immediately regretted calling him names. I apologized to him, but it was of no use. Hunter was so angry, he would not hear me. He just said, "Don't speak; I don't want to talk to you." That was it. Then we sat home without talking to each other. When it came time to go to bed, I went to sleep. The next day when I was about to go to work, I sat next to him on the bed. I told him that he didn't have to leave if he had no place to go. I had just been mad, the night before. He told me that he had a couple of places he could go, but he just hadn't figured out where he wanted to end up.

Hunter told me that he had quit his job the week before, and had told his employer that he was going to school.

Thursday night, he told me that he was leaving the next day. The next day, which was a Friday, Hunter asked me if he could drop me off at work so he could use the car to pick up his last paycheck. I told him to bring my car to my job during my lunch break, and I would take him to the bus station.

When Hunter came, he didn't have his bags with him. I thought it was strange but I didn't ask any questions. I felt that it was none of my business. Then, he told me that he was going to Boston, and when he comes back, he would leave our place. At that point, I didn't care.

When I got home from work, I found that he had packed all his stuff. I found out later that he had even packed the marriage certificate, although he said that the marriage didn't have any meaning for him. Oh well, he could have it. I didn't want it anyway at that time. Of course I was the one to go request and pay for a duplicate later.

Hunter left for Boston on a Friday and came back almost a week later. When he returned, we didn't talk. The next day was my day off, and I saw that he was packing the little stuff he had bought and he was spending time folding them a hundred times. He looked miserable like a child who didn't know what he was doing. I was about to leave with my roommate when I heard him asking her the number for a cab because he needed to go to the bank or something. My roommate is really soft-hearted. She asked me to give him my car. I felt that I was not going to offer something he didn't ask me for. But later, of course, I told him that if he needed to use a car he could take mine, and my roommate and I could use hers. I felt guilty afterwards; just because he was mean. I didn't have to be that same way. Probably he was ashamed to ask me for a ride knowing that he is leaving me, the time I needed him the most.

Later that day, he was trying to buy a bus ticket to go to his friend who was going to take him to the airport in Manchester. However, there was no bus going straight there. He would have to take a bus to Boston and from Boston take another one going to Manchester to his friend's house. This made the destination three times longer. But when his mission was not accomplished, he asked me if I could take him to his friend's place. I remember it was on November fourth around four in the afternoon. He took all his belongs, and I drove him to his friend.

On our way there Hunter asked, "Do you know where I am going?" I responded.

"How could I know? You never told me." I answered.

He said he was going to New York. He had a friend there. I didn't know this friend. I knew he had a friend in Canada and other friends in other states that he talked to. I never heard of a friend who lived in New York. But I didn't feel that I had the right to ask him questions at this point in our relationship. Besides I really didn't care that much to know. Five months ago, I was so eager to pick him up from the airport and so in love with him. But now I was sending him away.

When we got to the place he was staying overnight, I helped him get his bags out and carry them into the house. After that, he walked me to my car and thanked me for everything I had done for him. He told me to take care of myself and the baby. He added that we didn't have to be enemies because we never knew where life would take us. I couldn't believe my ears. It seemed like I was hearing someone else. Was this the same person who made my life a living hell for the last two months just because I was pregnant with his child? I said nothing except I wished him happiness in his life as well. Then I drove back home. It was a forty-five-minute drive, and it was dark which matched how I was feeling inside. I cried all the way home and began to face the reality that now he was gone and out of my life probably forever. I missed him and hated him at the same time. When I got home I expected to see him sitting on the couch he loved to sit on. But he wasn't.

After he left I cried myself to sleep for weeks. Sometimes I didn't think I could go on without him. I remember there was a white t-shirt he forgot to pack and I slept in it, only God knows how long. Sometimes I cursed myself for loving him so much without leaving a little piece for me to fall on, and for being weak. Why was I mourning for someone who didn't care? Other times, I blamed myself for him leaving me. I thought maybe if I had been normal and begged him to stay maybe he would have stayed. But other times, I thought that I didn't have to beg him. I deserved to be loved as much as I loved him. I didn't feel that it was right to beg him to stay and be in his son's life. It was his responsibility.

Before he left I gave him two gifts. One was a book called, "The Purpose Driven Life" and the other was the Bible. I was hoping that he would read them and not throw them away. Every day I prayed that he would open his heart to God and let Him help him deal with all his issues. He had to face his demons. Even though I had not come to terms with God, I knew that the consequences I was facing were directly related to my actions.

Chapter 25

"Have mercy on me, O God, according to your unfailing love; according to your great compassion blot out my trans-aggressions. Wash away all my iniquity and cleanse me from my sin."

~ Psalms 51:1-2

After Hunter left, I knew that I needed to change my life and the way I had been living. I knew that all my life I had tried to control my life without God, and with every attempt, I lost. I was so tired of running and running and falling on my face all the time. I saw my separation from Hunter as an eye-opening experience for me and a new beginning. I prayed to God to guide my life and to help me stay in His presence. I know, without Him in my life, I am completely helpless. Besides, what was I going to teach my child if I didn't have my act together? What kind of mother was I going to be? What kind of legacy was I going to leave my child? I never dreamed about being a single mother, never mind being one who was left alone while still pregnant. I couldn't imagine how I was going to do it without the father of my child. I prayed God would guide me and protect me through the entire journey.

I prayed that Hunter would turn his heart to God and realize that he was not running away from anyone except himself. I knew that sometimes when we do bad things or make wrong choices, we get to the point where we see that there is no way we can turn back or be forgiven. I could remember after he told me that he wanted nothing to do with the baby that I told him he should do the right thing.

Afterward, he was like… "What do you want me to do… go and marry every woman I have hurt?"

At the time, I looked at this statement as an excuse to escape his responsibility. But then I wondered if that's what he really believed— that there is no way he could right the wrongs in his life. How long is he going to run? How long is he going to be hurt? How long is he going to hurt others just because he made mistakes during his life… things that he believes he cannot undo? I wish he knew this was a lie from hell. I believe and know that there is always hope in Jesus. No matter what we do, God forgives us. To be able to enjoy that forgiveness, we must be willing to accept it and forgive ourselves as well. There is nothing too hard or too dirty for Jesus. He carries all our mistakes, selfishness, bad choices on Him; and 'by his wounds we are healed'.

The first thing I needed was to move out of the apartment we were living in. I needed to get out of that place because every time I entered that house, all I heard was Hunter's voice and the drama that took place in that house. The good things that happened there made me cry and I missed him so much, but the bad times made me hate him. It had become clear I needed a different environment.

Right after he left, I started going to church again. As hard it was to go back, I felt that there was no way I would be able to survive the stress I was going through without going to church. I was praying and hoping that God would forgive me and that I would allow me to feel His peace and presence all around me again. And He did. However, some days were still hard.

———

I remember one day, I was sitting in church, during morning service. People were singing and praising God. All of a sudden, I felt so much rage and bitterness toward Hunter. The pain was so great I couldn't breathe. I cried for about twenty minutes. During that service, I couldn't pray or sing. I felt so alone and had so much anger toward Hunter. I was wondering about how he could do that to me. How was I going to raise this child alone? Misery kept creeping into my heart, and I felt sick. I was nauseous and wanted to throw up. My pain was so uncontrollable, I asked God to help me not to hate him. I asked for His forgiveness, and to my surprise, I prayed for Hunter and really meant it. I prayed that God would touch my pain and suffering within me and turn it into glorifying His name. I asked God to give me peace of mind. I knew regardless of how I felt, I had to think about my baby because my little one depended upon me staying healthy and being able to keep my positive thinking. I felt that even though I didn't know what lay ahead, what I knew was that whatever my future was, my child and I were in the Almighty's hands. After this incident, I went on with my life and God truly gave me peace.

Although God had given me peace of mind, sometimes the hatred for Hunter would rise up. I continued to ask God to help me to forgive him completely..

Throughout my pregnancy it was love and hate days. Even, someday I prayed and hoped that my child will not look like his father. I felt that I would not be able to take it if people said, "Oh, my goodness, he looks like Hunter." I have never told anyone about all these things that are inside of me, now. But this is what was on my mind.

One day after church, I was at Christina' house, and I was feeling sorry for myself, whining about how I was going to have to raise this child by myself, and as always, my sister told me the family will always be there for me and the baby. For the first time, I told her how I hated Hunter so much to the point it made me want to throw up. She said that for a while she thought I was not normal because I had never reacted to his leaving. Then she told me that my feelings were normal, and that I just had to be honest with God and tell Him how I felt. She said that I should try to pray for Hunter every time that hate rises up and ask God to bless him. Sometimes I do but if I am being honest I am not completely there yet. Maybe someday I will think his name without some bad thoughts going behind it.

My sister told me that if I didn't pray and forgive Hunter, that hatred could hinder my relationship with God, and it would not be good for my baby. I believed what she told me, but I wondered how long it would take for me to live my life in peace. It astonishes me how I can miss Hunter miserably and detest him at the same time. I don't even know if I have ever hated anyone as much as I hated him. Even my feelings for the people who killed my whole family doesn't come close to how I sometimes felt about him.

Chapter 26

"If we confess our sins, he is faithful and just and will forgive us our sins and purify us from all unrighteousness"

1 John 1:9

Eventually, I asked my roommate if we could find another apartment. Genie told me that she didn't like changes. I didn't blame her. We had a beautiful apartment, and our landlord was awesome. We were probably not going to find another one like it. I told her to find another person to live with because I couldn't live there anymore. Soon, she found a woman who was very nice. I was glad that Genie found a nice roommate. When she came to see the house, she said I didn't have to move.

Genie offered to help me during my pregnancy by allowing us to live with them without having to pay rent. For a while they convinced me, and it was tempting to stay with them because they were a lot of fun. But after I thought about it, I knew if I stayed in that house, my life would never change. I needed something more than just those girls. I needed God in my life to help me, and if I stayed in that apartment, there was going to be only unresolved grief and bitterness. I needed God and needed strong believers around me who would help me to get back to my first love and these girls were not going to give me that.

I didn't think living by myself was a good idea either. I needed people to give me encouragement. At the same time, I didn't want to go back home to my sister after two years of living on my own, plus... I didn't want anyone to feel sorry for me and I am being honest, I don't think she wanted this chaotic and emotional rollercoaster around her or the girls either. She had done enough and this was my burden to carry. I prayed hard for God to give me a solution. While I was having this mind battle, I had a good friend who was so wonderful to me through all my drama. She beseeched me to go live with her and her family. They were so excited and wanted me to come live with them. I told them to give me time, but in my heart, I knew that I needed another place to stay. My friend and her family were absolutely amazing, kind and loving but I needed people who were grounded in Christ, to help me strengthen my faith and relationship with Jesus. I needed someone who could help me only I didn't know who. Then out of nowhere, I thought about a couple at my church. They were a wonderful Christian family. I knew if I went to live with them it would be a blessing to me, and my life needed that.

I told my sister, and she thought that it was a good idea. I was afraid to go and ask them, even though they knew my entire situation. I asked Christina to go with me, but she insisted I should do it by myself. But I knew she would come anyway when the time came to ask them. After service that Sunday I asked the lady of the house. Her name was Cyndie. She told me that actually she and her husband had been wondering if I wanted to come and live with them. She said they had been praying about it and was going to ask me if I would like to go live with them. Do you see how awesome God is? He is intentional and does things on our behalf. even when we think there is nothing going on Jesus is working behind the scene. Then Cyndie told me she would talk to her husband and give me a response by the night service. She was confident though that her husband would say *yes*. Later they told me I could come and live with them, which seemed to be an answer to my prayer.

A week later, Cyndie came and told me that my room was now ready for me. I hesitated because even though I asked, I was nervous. I kept telling them I needed to pack and would let them know when I was ready.

Then, one Friday in the middle of November, Craig, Cyndie's husband, called me and told me that they were coming to pick up some of my stuff. They came one day and moved my bedroom set and my furniture in one round. Since I had no choice I had to follow them. I didn't even have a chance to say *goodbye* to my roommate because she was at work. By the time I got to Craig and Cyndie's house, everything was all set up and put away. I didn't have to do anything. I couldn't believe the kindness of these people.

When I got there, they had literally created a studio look-alike room for me, down in their large basement. The space they created looked nice and big enough for my entire bedroom and couch. Plus, in front of it there was a beautiful big new bathroom. It was so amazing that I just wanted to cry after I saw it. Living with this family was a blessing to me. It helped me restore my relationship with God in my life, and the move helped me put my life back in line. Even though they already had four kids of their own, they were excited to receive my baby as one of their own.

After moving in with this family, I really didn't think about Hunter that much because they helped me to heal. Never hearing from him helped me as well. After he left, I never heard from him for about a month. I didn't mind about that either because I was busy trying to adjust to my new life.

Nonetheless, after forty-five days without hearing anything from Hunter, I started wondering if he was okay. I prayed for him every day and hoped he was fine. Time to time, I wanted to send him an email to see if he was alright, but I didn't and decided to leave him alone. In the meantime, his driving license arrived at our previous address. I guess, before he left he applied for it. But, because he was not an American citizen, he got a temporary license for forty-five days before they sent the actual license in the mail. So, when my former roommate got it in the mail, she called me asking me what she should do with it.

"I think your husband's license came, so what do you want me to do with it?" she asked.

Unbelievable! I was still called his wife, even though he was gone and didn't claim me as his wife. Up to this day, people still call me to tell me what my husband did or said. It always makes me wonder how long it will take people to realize that I am not attached to him anymore.

Anyway, I went to pick up Hunter's license. That night I sent him an email telling him that I had his driver's license. After that email, I didn't hear from him for two weeks. I thought maybe he didn't need it. Then a few days before Christmas, he called and left a message telling me to send it to him as soon as I could because he really needed it. He left his address, but I really didn't understand it. I called the number on my caller id, but no one answered. I tried a couple times, and then I gave up. I knew if he really needed his license, he would call me. The next morning, he called. It was so strange talking to him after all that time.

I couldn't believe he was still the same. He went on talking about himself. All I could hear was his arrogance and pride. I just listened to him talking and wondered when he was going to get over himself. He asked me if I could send his license overnight. It was always about him. He didn't even ask me how I was doing or where I was living. What if I had no money to send it express, what if I was sick and couldn't work because of the pregnancy?

The good news was that through this phone call it was clear he no longer had power over me. I could do whatever I wanted and it was not up to him. After ten or fifteen minutes of talking, I felt that our conversation was empty. I couldn't believe how things had changed. This was the man I used to love and adore, but now, hearing his voice felt strange to me. That day I went to work and on my way, I thought about sending him his license but I decided against it. I went to work. Since his birthday is on December 24th, I bought him a card to wish him a happy birthday and a Merry Christmas. I put the license inside the card and sent it by regular mail the next day.

He never called me to tell me he got the license. But I knew he got it, because if he didn't, he would have called. I prayed to God to help me to just try to forget him and go on without him ruining my mind. I had to have peace of mind for my child's sake.

I don't know what was it about this guy, but when I was trying to live and just have my own life, there were always people telling me about him, which didn't help. They would say, "I saw Hunter working at this place, Hunter this and Hunter that." I decided to cut people off and just talked to the few that I knew would not talk about him or ask me questions about him. Still, there was always something about Hunter that came up no matter what. By the end of December, my former roommate got another letter for Hunter. It was a letter from immigration telling him to come for the interview for his permanent residency. It was the final interview. The letter also stated I had to go with him.

I didn't know that we had to go for an interview because in the last notice they had stated that they were reviewing his papers and would send him a letter in the mail with their decision. I think when he left, he didn't think he was going to need me for anything.

When I got that letter, I didn't bother to write or send him an email to tell him. I just forwarded it to him and waited to see what he was going to do. After that, he didn't call to tell me anything about it, and I didn't call either to see if he got it. I really didn't care.

After Hunter left, people were telling me that I needed to divorce him and tell immigration that he used me so they could send him back home. But I didn't want to do that. Besides everything I was going through was new to me, and I was trying to figure out what had happened. The last thing on my mind was going through all that drama again. I also thought that sending him back home would be revenge, and in my heart, I knew that I didn't want revenge.

I knew all these people cared and loved me to the point that if I had given some of them permission to write or call immigration, they would have done it. But I had to stand my ground and I told them that it was not up to any of us to make that decision to send him home. I felt that I was the one who struggled to bring him here, so no one had the right to tell me what to do. One of my good friends was so concerned that I was going to get in trouble if the immigration found out that Hunter and I were not living together anymore. She called a lawyer/friend of hers to ask him for advice. All these people had good intentions, but they didn't look beyond me. They were so concerned about me without thinking about the baby I was carrying inside of me.

As evil as he seemed to be, Hunter was still the father of my child. I couldn't do such a thing just because he had hurt me. How could I have lived with myself knowing that one-day my child would grow up and ask me questions about his father? And then I would have to tell him that I shipped him back to Rwanda. What if something happened to him there? Would I be able to forgive myself? I knew how sad it is to grow up without a father. It is better to have a wicked one around than not to have one at all. Everything I was doing I always did thinking about my baby. I know how hard my teenage years were without both my parents and wished they had been around. So, I didn't want to do the same thing to my baby.

Every day I dedicated my baby's life to God and prayed that he would grow up to be a man of God, respected by everyone because of his good character. I hope he will make a difference in people's lives and that God would help me to never teach him evil ways.

Finally, I overcame this battle of people telling me what to do. When the letter came, it reminded me of everything I had been going through and I wondered if I was going to get in trouble. Sometimes I tried to believe in my heart that Hunter didn't come to the US just for papers. Then again, maybe he was just selfish and didn't want any responsibility and decided to run away; if you think about it... two years... it is not a long time to wait for papers if that's why he came here. I tried to see some goodness in him, even though it is hard.

After I sent the immigration letter to Hunter quite a bit of time passed with me not hearing from him. Then, on New Year's Eve day just after midnight, he called me and told me that he was calling to wish me a Happy New Year, *yeah sure*, rolled my eyes in my mind! Hunter stated that he got the letter I sent to him from immigration. After a couple minutes, I wished him a Happy New Year, thanked him for calling and hung up the phone. Later that night, when I was lying in bed, I wondered if he did really care about me. At least he had called to wish me a Happy New Year. Possibly, Hunter didn't have any other way to approach me to tell me about the letter and he had decided to use that strategy to mention it. Anything was possible when it came to my man, I couldn't trust him.

After that call on New Year's Eve, I didn't hear from him again for a while. Then, during the middle of January, he called. I was running late to go pick up a kid from school that I was babysitting that week because his parents were at a conference. When my cellphone rang, I picked it up without even looking at who was calling. When I heard Hunter's voice, I wished I hadn't taken the call. I was not in the mood to talk to him. I asked him what he wanted and then he went on with this small talk that didn't even make sense at all. He said something was going to come to my ex-roommate's house and asked if I could send them back to him. Hunter always called me just to get me to do something for him, never to just check on me. For the first time in our relationship, I told him *no* and asked him why he couldn't call my ex-roommate and do it for himself?

Our conversation went on and on so, finally, I said I would do it just to get him to leave me alone. Then, I realized that he had called to ask about the immigration interview, but he didn't know how to start the conversation about it without stupid excuses. At the end he said, "About the interview… are you coming with me or what?" Just like that. He never had any respect or politeness in his demands. I thought in my head how arrogant he was, but I didn't say it aloud; it didn't matter anymore. I told him that I had no choice, since I had never told them that we were separated. I felt that it was my obligation to go and tell them what was happening. I asked him how he was going to explain to immigration why he was now living in New York. Hunter said he was going to tell them that he was training for a truck driving job. I wanted to laugh, but I didn't.

His stupid lies always amazed me. I asked, "Do you think that it would be right to lie to them?"

"Why not?" he asked.

I gave up and told him to call back; I had to go. Before I hung up though, I told him that I was having a boy because I had found out the day before he called. This made me happy because I wanted a boy with all my heart. God had answered my prayers. I didn't want to have a girl because I worried that having a girl meant she might have to go through similar things, which had happened to me. When I told him the baby's gender, he was not expecting to hear that. He choked. I could hear him. He froze for about a minute, and then he said, "Thanks."

I wanted to ask him, "Thanks for what?" But I didn't waste my breath. Instead, I hung up and thought about how he didn't even ask me what I was going to say in the interview.

After that call, I went on with my life. I lived one day at a time. He really underestimated and took me for granted and was always so sure that I was there to serve him. My friend Lonzen would always tell me that that's not a way to live. Sometimes, I felt like an unbeliever. I didn't see the reason of planning anything anymore because who knows what the future might bring? You plan and things don't work out as you hoped. So, what's the use of planning? This philosophy of mine could save me a lot of disappointment. But I knew better, God is the planner and I should live according to His will. Lonzen and Fidelis were two friends that I really cherished. They were the ones who kept me going when I was pregnant. Not one day passed without one of them calling to check on me. And what made them special was when they called me; they called expressing concern about me and not about them. They actually cared about me. Their phone calls came without gossip, too. Calls from these two friends came with just laughter, sometimes-stupid jokes, dumb conversations and inspiration all at the same time; each one had a special meaning in my life. Fidelis was my talking buddy and my protective big brother. He calmed my soul. It's so funny how he used to get so mad at me when I did something of which he didn't approve. He was the best older brother I never had and confidant.

Lonzen was my inspiration. Lonzen was a dreamer. He always encouraged me to do things sometimes I didn't have the guts to do. When he found out that I was pregnant and Hunter had left me, he thought my life was going to be over. He had the crazy idea of taking my child to live with his mother after I had the baby. We talked about our goals in life. We all had this crazy idea of making a difference in people's lives. He knew my hopes and dreams, and I knew his. He was going to be a lawyer and have a doctorate degree. I was going to have a Ph.D. in Psychology specializing in Posttraumatic Stress Disorder so we could go home and help our people in Rwanda. All those dreams changed a lot. He did have a Ph.D. but never got his law degree. About my degree probably someday when all my children are grown and need something to do, I might go and get my doctorate but for now, I am just happy with my Masters in Mental Health Counseling.

So, when I was pregnant, Lonzen looked at it as though my dreams had died. But what Lonzen did not see was that I could still see my dream as being added on to, with a blessing from God, a gift of a child I never dreamed I would have.

Lonzen went behind my back and asked his mother if she could take my baby and raise him. His mother is as generous as he is. She agreed to do it without even knowing me. He told me that his mother was excited about raising my child. His plan was for me to go with the baby to Rwanda after I gave birth. Stay with the baby in Rwanda for a couple of months. Then come back and continue my life.

Lonzen said, "You could go see him during your vacations or call him anytime. It will be like leaving your baby with your mother."

His caring was meaningful to me – it was very nice and thoughtful of him but I had to turn down the offer. I told him that I couldn't do it even if it was going to be hard to raise my son alone, but after all we had gone through together, there is no way I could send him away. I couldn't let anybody raise him except me. This was the reason I adored my friends. I could never have asked more.

When the immigration interview got closer, I was nervous and wondered what I would be able to say. One of my questions was - will I get in trouble if they find out as the people were telling me? Hunter never called again to talk about what would happen either. I made up my mind that even though I would not call immigration to tell them he was not living with me, I knew if they asked about it, I was not going to lie. I didn't see any reason to lie; there is never a reason for lying anyway.

Deep down in my heart I always hoped Hunter would come to his senses and apologize for all the horrible things he said to me so we could raise our baby together. I also thought that it was not right to rush making a decision to separate permanently because you never know what the future might bring. I didn't think that every couple who separated automatically filed for divorce. Divorce was the last thing on my mind.

I was still shocked about being a pregnant single mother. I never dreamed that such a predicament could happen to me. Call me a *dreamer* for wishing him to come back to me, but I never wanted or wished to raise a child alone. I believe every child deserves to have parents, a mom and a dad. That is how I was raised, and I always appreciated each of them and wanted my child to have the same. I never wished to have a child who would always be wishing that his father was there. Early on in our separation, I dreamt that someday he would return to me. Probably reading too many romance novels as a teenager was influencing my thoughts. I even had a scenario in my head about how he was going to come back and beg me to forgive him. Thank God no one knew about my silly dream. My tears came every day for God to give Hunter a change of heart so he would come back into our lives. For His good reason that dream or prayer never came true.

At some point, it hit Hunter that he hadn't talked to me about what I was going to say at the immigration interview. He called and left me a message that we needed to talk. However, I didn't call him back. I didn't want to talk to him. But I knew soon enough I would hear from him again. When it comes to what he wanted Hunter had persistence. The next day he called, but I was not in the mood to talk to him. So, I didn't answer his call. After he called maybe three times, I decided to return his call and see what he wanted, even though I knew what he wanted. He was never persuasive until he wanted something. I was at work at the time the phone rang. This time, he called and talked to me as if he cared. Hunter's first question was to ask me where I was living since he noticed that I had a different address. How come he never asked me about these matters before.

Throughout our conversation, he never once asked about the baby. I guess that was still an untouchable subject. He went around in circles without him telling me the real reason he called. Later during our call, he asked me about the upcoming interview. Hunter admitted that he was wondering what was going to happen and questioned what we were going to say. All of sudden, "he and I" became "we."

How nice. I told Hunter that I was going to tell the truth at the interview. He asked me why I was going to tell the truth. Again, he told me that I should tell them that he was living in New York because he was being trained for a truck-driving job. I was so aggravated, but what made me even more frustrated was talking to someone who didn't think about anyone else but himself.

After a while, the conversation was going nowhere. I told him not to worry that they would not send him home because I was pregnant with his child. I said this even though I was not sure about that. I told him that unless he didn't think that this child was his, then there was nothing else I could do about it. Actually, though, I just said that to provoke him. I even told Hunter that I knew he never wanted a son, but I was not going to say that at the interview. Nor had my plans included telling them any of the other horrible things he had said to me. I had no interest in whether he got his papers or not.

"Who said that I didn't want this child?" he asked. I wanted to scream, but I just ignored him. Either he was sick or had developed short-term memory. However, because he didn't have any power over what I should say or not say, Hunter had to come to the interview. He didn't have a choice. At the end of our call he told me that he would call me.

Even though most people believe that Hunter never intended to come here just for me, I tried to believe that he moved to US not just for the paperwork. If it was only that he would have waited to make sure he got them, which was not a long wait. At that time, probably he was confused — I could not wish to be in his shoes. How could you sleep at night knowing that out there, there was a child that belonged to you and you had forsaken him? Sometimes I tried to excuse his behavior in my mind.

The interview day came. It was on Monday. He called me on Thursday and told me that he was coming on Friday night. He was staying at his friend's house near where the interview was going to be. When he arrived Friday around one in the morning, he called me. However, I did not pick up my phone. The nerve of him to call me that late like I was one of his friends, who was eager to know he was back in town. He called again the next night, but again, I didn't take his call.

About six in the morning on Sunday he called again. I couldn't believe him! I just looked at his number in shock. He left a sad voice message that said, "I have been trying to call you, but I do not know why I cannot find you." Listening to that voice of his, I felt disgusted. He was probably scared that I would not show up for the interview or he might have been worried about what I was going to say if I showed up at all.

It's funny, when I was pregnant, one minute I could be praying for him and then one minute I could be so mad at him. Oh goodness, hormones are so confusing.

The week Hunter came, it was not the best time for me. After I got his message, I decided to text him back at seven. Because I didn't feel like talking to him, I told him that there were days when I was so mad at him; and that this day happened to be one of those that I was angry. So as not to be too confusing, I told him that I had received all his messages, but I was still not in the mood to talk. "Hunter, do you want me to tell you that I am excited that you came? If that is the case… then, no, I am not. That was a different person who used to feel that way, now I have changed. I promised you that I would be at the interview, then I would be there." After my text messages, I didn't hear from him all day.

That Sunday night, he called again. My phone was under my niece Gabriella's leg. It was on vibrate, she jumped and gave me an evil look that seemed to say, "What does Hunter ant or why are you talking to him?" When I got home, it was after nine in the evening. I called him, and Hunter picked up on the first ring, He asked if my phone was working. I told him it was working fine and asked him if he had gotten my message. Hunter lied and said that he hadn't because his phone had not been charged.

I explained that I had sent the text messages that morning after he called me. He asked what it was about. I told him that I am sure he knew but, I was coming to the interview the next day. I didn't feel that I needed to explain information he already knew.

Hunter said if he had received my message, he would not have kept trying to call me. I really disliked his little games. After all the nonsensical conversation we hung up.

Chapter 27

"But you, Lord, are a shield around me, my glory, the one who lifts my head high"

~ Psalms 3:3

The next day I went to the interview, but because I didn't want to go by myself, my friends Craig and Cyndie came with me. I didn't want to face Hunter alone. I knew him, and I knew myself as well. Even though I acted tough, I also realized my weakness when it came him. When we got there, he was outside waiting. Because Hunter was expecting to see my car, he didn't notice that we were there until I was about to get out of the car. Because there were others with me, he came toward me acting like he was happy to see me. I felt anger rising inside of me. Maybe he could sense this and reached out and gave me a hug. Instead of pulling away, I gave him a hug back, but without a smile. I just wanted to tell him, "Let's just go… so, I can get over with this." All I could feel at that moment was the pain that he had caused me.

I bottled all of those feelings and went into the interview with him. Before the interview when had been sitting down; Hunter spoke about what the immigration people were going to ask us. I guess this was another tactic to convince me, that I shouldn't say anything about our marital status. As he talked, I felt nauseous. I wanted to scream at him to shut up, because he was making me angry enough to feel sick. I couldn't stand his voice anymore to the point that I had to go to the bathroom and ask God to help me get through this. I was thinking probably this would be the last time I had to deal with him. After my emotions calmed down, I went back, sat next to him and told him that I was not going to lie no matter what.

After a few minutes the officer came out in the hall and called his name. When Hunter rose to follow the officer, he looked so nervous. Naturally, I followed along with them. The officer asked us to stand and raise our right hands to swear that we would tell the truth. After we all sat down, the officer of the immigration verified our phone numbers and address. He went on to ask Hunter if he had committed any crime and other questions about drugs and so on. I was sitting there, and the man never asked me anything. He informed us that the income I had submitted for last year's tax return didn't meet the requirements. I explained I was in school but that I had given them the statement for that year. He said they still needed more income unless I had done the 2005 tax return. I told him than I hadn't done those yet.

Turning to Hunter, the man said, "Hunter, we need you to bring six pay stubs and then we'll approve the case." He also stated that in two weeks Hunter would get his card in the mail.

After all the information was given, the interview was over. We got up, thanked the officer and then we left the room. When we got outside, you could see that Hunter could not believe that I hadn't said anything. He tried to hug me, and he thanked me. But I was not in the mood. Then I went to the car and headed home.

The truth was that I felt during the interview, that I had no reason to stop the officer and say, "Hold on officer, I don't see the point of this interview. This man left me pregnant and we no longer live together. As a matter fact, he lives in another state and I haven't seen him in three months." I felt doing that would not have brought him back to me. Nor would it take away all the pain I was carrying inside of me. Although, as much as Hunter had hurt me, I didn't want him to get deported. If that became the outcome of all this it would mean that my child would never see Hunter until he was all grown up. That's the reason I was giving myself... in my mind, much less to keep the details to myself. However, sometimes I wonder if I attended the interview and kept my mouth shut for my son's sake or for myself by hoping that maybe just maybe someday Hunter would change and return to us and be united with his family again. *A girl can dream and hope.* After that interview, he went his way and I went mine. I didn't hear from him... not even a phone call. Sometime I couldn't believe he was really gone. In my late pregnancy when the baby was active and kicking, I wondered how it would have been if his father was still there with me.

Sometimes I got angry at him for stealing the joy of being pregnant. I always dreamed of having my baby's father around and would be excited for the coming of our first child. Don't get me wrong, I love my child. I know and believe that nothing makes me happier than this child. But sometimes I wonder what it would have been like if his father had embraced the news positively and stayed by my side. I knew Hunter would have been a wonderful father if he had given this child a chance, because I know how affectionate he can be.

The first few weeks after Hunter arrived from Rwanda, it was like a honeymoon. He cooked and sometimes even brought me breakfast in the bed. At that time, I couldn't ask for any better man than him. I thought he was perfect. Every day I thought I was the luckiest woman in the world, even though in the end, he turned into another creature. Sometimes I ask myself why I never saw the signs of his true color. Now I know the truth was hurtful, sad and pitiful as it may sound. I was so desperate for love I saw what I wanted to see. If I had been honest to myself, obedience to God and people who love me, I would not have been involved in this relationship in the first place.

I tried to believe maybe Hunter didn't mean everything he said to me. Or maybe I didn't want to believe that I had fallen in love with the wrong man. Did the man I loved really not love me? How about the little things he used to do for me to make me happy? Had it all been an act? I wanted to believe that Hunter would not have done those little things if he had not cared about me. I still believed that by God's loving hand and mercy, he could turn around and see that being a dad is not a bad thing. Actually, I believed that it could cure him of his tormented past.

Chapter 28

"I will give you a new heart and put a new
spirit in you; I will remove from you your heart
of stone and give you a heart of flesh."

~ Ezekiel 36:26

When I was pregnant I would sit and look at my beautiful nieces and pray that they would see that the world is full of pain, sufferings and sins, which they should never be fooled by. Hopefully, they would never repeat the same mistakes I had. I prayed to God that if I had to have a painful life to teach a lesson to them, let that be. Or, if my life could be a testimony to someone who needed their life changed my pain would be worth it. Still, I didn't want to see them get hurt or go through what I have gone through because of my rebelliousness and didn't listen to my sister or other people God has put in my life to guide me. I was defiant and listened to my flesh instead of listening to the word of God. I never committed my life fully to God. I had one foot in the world and the other in the Word. Therefore, there had been a great price to pay. I learned the hard way. The pleasures of the world come for a short time, but the pain can be great and last forever. Now, when I look at all this pain, it doesn't seem worth it.

When you grow up in a Christian home, you are so vulnerable. The world swallows you alive, and you go around thinking that you know a lot. But you don't. I wish I never had had to learn by experiencing the price and pain of sin. I used to think some of what we learned in church or the things my sister used to tell me was overboard. My thoughts were that everything could not be as bad as they had made it seem. I rebelled against what I was taught. Being naïve, I thought that I knew better and was old enough to know what was right and wrong. I didn't see how going to clubs could be wrong if I didn't drink or didn't do anything wrong while there. However, as they say, your eyes are the window to your soul. They are right because even if you go with the right heart, pretty soon what you see or hear, you want to experience. Later, you find yourself thinking things you never thought you could think, and those thoughts replace God's thoughts or at least ones He would have you think. Soon afterward what follows are the actions. Before I fornicated, I used to think that if I ever did it, my sister and everyone I passed that day would know I had been with a man. I thought I would never be able to go in front of God and pray. That thought kept me away from sinning for a long time until I was surrounded by people who thought there was nothing wrong with our behavior. Pretty soon, I found myself dreaming to see how it felt. All those stupid thoughts drove me to have a boyfriend when I shouldn't have, because I wanted to experience what I was missing.

Satan has a sneaky way of manipulating innocent Christian girls and showing them that the men they are dating would be their husbands someday — so, there was nothing wrong with what they were doing then or in what they would do sooner or later. This is a lie from hell because the different between husband/wife vs fiancé/boyfriend uniting as one; the first union was ordained by God; God has blessed and breathed a life through this relationship, the other one… the devil has blessed, breathed lies and death through it. unless by the Grace of God, He chose to keep you together because of his unending mercy. There is no guarantee that a boyfriend or fiancé will end up becoming your husband. Look at me, I had two serious relationships and none of them became permanent husbands. My stupidity didn't help me to keep my purity. I sold out cheap what was valued and pleasured by God. When you sin for the first time, you feel guilty, but after a while, it becomes normal, and that was my game. Two weeks of guiltiness and maybe a month of good. Hopefully my nieces had learned from me and would stay under the wings of the Lord.

In addition, for me, Satan had a lot of things he used to do to keep me from serving God. I never surrounded my pain totally to God. "What's the point of staying sexually pure; it's not like you are a virgin?" The enemy will whisper in my ears. Rape is one of the worst things that can happen to any human being; the pain of it destroys the core of your being, you feel your whole existence and sense of worth decaying every single day. Unless the Almighty Jehovah Rapha touches you and heals you from the deepest of your soul; the alternative is to end your life or self-medicated with drugs, alcohol or men to ease your pain or cause you to feel numb. Unfortunately, I chose self-medicating by running to find my sense of worth in men. I thought it was too impossible for God to take my pain away. Although I completely forgave the people who killed my family and violated me. I never gave my pain and self-loathing to God. "How can anyone heal the scar of my soul? How could I explain to someone that I am rotting away inside to the point sometimes I wanted to end my life; who has that kind of power to do that?"

That's the lie the enemy kept me under for decades. I always felt insecure and felt that I could never be loved by anybody. I felt that if a guy loved me, it was because he was feeling sorry for me and I was being given a favor. The devil used my painful past as a target which was hard not to do. I was an emotional wreck even though I acted tough outside. During my bad days I could still smell the odor of the man who had violated me. Somedays I couldn't eat because my nausea was so strong. I was convinced that no one could ever love me. My assurance was that if a guy could love me maybe then I was alright. I nursed my pain, and it was also sugarcoated with the devil's tactics. Instead of surrendering my pain to God, I lived a double life. If I had totally given my life over to God, God would have restored me and taken that pain away, but I made wrong choices again and again. I sought healing and comfort from broken men like me, one who didn't have anything better to offer me but even more pain. Then I paid the price because everything we do has consequences good or bad. Thank God. He is a God of second chances. He is a long-suffering God and never gives up on us as the world does. He will wait until you realize that He has been there all long.

I hope and pray that God will help me to be a good mother. I know my family and friends will help me through all my difficulties. I hope Hunter someday will see the love of God and he will learn being a father is a privilege and a blessing that should not be taken for granted. I hope he will learn that giving a child anything he wants without love means nothing. Material things are meaningless.

I believe rejecting your child is a terrible thing. He didn't give me a chance to show him that there is another way to feel love, the love of your children. I believe God loves Hunter more than I do. His timing is not my timing; I pray that God will give him a gift of salvation before he dies that He has granted me. I can't worry so much for him though. I have so much I have to learn from God I need to focus more on my salvation and let my redeemer align my thinking with his thought toward me. Most of what I thought I knew was entwined with the lie of the enemy.

People see me as a woman who has been used and manipulated, but that's not how I see myself. I see wake-up calls and that God has given me a second chance to live for only Him. God used different things for each of us to bring us back to Him and remind us who we belong to; mine was showing me that meaningless relationships will never heal my pain but only bring more misery. Only true healing comes from the One who created me — He knows what makes me whole.

I just hope through this child, Hunter will change himself and live life without the insecurity of people leaving him or not loving him enough. Then, someday, he will not be afraid of commitment to someone he has fallen in love with. Hunter doesn't trust anyone, because the most important people in his life hurt him. But God could heal him if only Hunter would let Him in. I believe if God had given me these chances, then, who am I to judge anyone? I didn't see why I couldn't give Hunter a chance to know his child. I pray that he should grow to love our son and see that it was not bad or too hard to be a father after all. I missed him so much, and sometimes, I wished he could come back to me. But I came to realize that it's not up to me. I really care more about his heart and wish he could live his life without holding onto things that hurt him in his past.

We all have some kind of traumatic past event we could hold onto if we wanted to ruin our lives. For example, I could dwell on my painful experiences during the genocide; but, I know I would have a nervous breakdown every month. That's why I now choose to live my life without thinking too much about it. Each day I lay my pain in the hands of God. It doesn't mean I forget about my family or what has happened to me. It's just that I made the decision with God's help to live beyond my pain.

One friend of mine told me that my life was like a Hollywood story, that he has never heard of a Rwandan woman who married and separated in five months. Sometimes I could not believe that our relationship was over in that short a time, either. There were times when I wondered if Hunter ever really existed in my life or if it was a nightmare like so many I have of my past. However, always I am reminded of the reality of it by a kick in the guts; "hello back to earth mother" said my son in the womb. I wished Hunter would have realized I was afraid also about having a baby. Since our son was conceived out of love (I think?!?), I saw my child as a gift from above. When the baby kicked, it made me happy knowing that he was alive and well and happy to play with mommy sometimes or the least remind me what's coming. I was very grateful to God for that. I saw my child as the best thing that had happened for both of us, and I hoped that his father would find comfort in his son as I did. He is the joy of my life.

There is a song we sing at our church that says, "It's you, Lord, who came to save, the heart and soul of every man. It's you, Lord, who knows my weakness who gives me strength with thy own hand. Lead me, Lord, from temptation, purify me from within. Fill my heart with your Holy Spirit take away all my sins." This song gives me hope and comfort in knowing that God is on my side. He knows that I am not perfect. No matter what I go through in life, He will always be on my side and ready to forgive me and protect me as long as I don't abuse this amazing love He has given all of humankind. Also my child has given me the strength I never realized existed… not in my life, anyway. God has made me look at my life through a microscope and investigate my life as a clear picture with all the details.

After I did that, I didn't like what I saw. I decided to surrender my life, my pain and my sin with no turning back. The bible says, "Weeping may remain for the night, but joy will come in the morning." I believe this with all my heart because no matter how much I feel inside, I know this child will bring joy to my life. I have changed through this pregnancy. I knew that when my son was born, he would meet a new me and I was so excited because I wanted to be a wonderful mother to this baby who God had blessed me with. I know it is hard to be a single mother, but I know I have this close relationship with God, knowing that He loves me more than I love this child.

I believe that there is nothing I cannot do with Him. He will give me wisdom in raising my son. There is another song that says, "Under your wings I hide and I will not be afraid. You are the strength of my life, oh, Lord…." What should I worry about when I have this assurance of knowing that the "joy of the Lord will be our strengths?"

The power that raised Jesus Christ from the dead lives in me. God is on our side. I also pray that Hunter will come to realize what he is missing, and come to his senses and that he will try to be in his son's life. I believe this will help him as well. I am not bitter and I don't hate him anymore. I am just disappointed and I pray to God every day to take this disappointment from me. If God could forgive me, and show no disappointment toward me, who am I to judge or not forgive others?

Chapter 29

"The LORD your God is in your midst, a mighty one who will save; he will rejoice over you with gladness; he will quiet you by his love; he will exult over you with loud singing."

~ Zephaniah 3:17

In the last term of my pregnancy I felt miserable and unable to feel the excitement most women talk about experiencing during their last months. Most of the time, I was feeling sorry for myself. There was this lonely sad feeling inside my heart. I was ashamed for being pregnant and hated myself for it. Always, I wished for this feeling to go away. This feeling was so strong it made me worried that I would not be a good mother, and it even tried to convince me that I did not love my baby. There were times I didn't think I was going to give my son all the love he deserved. It took me a long time to realize that it was the devil messing with my mind, which was not hard to do in my condition.

Besides, not feeling loving, I also felt so ugly and fat to the point I didn't want to look at myself in the mirror anymore. There was a mirror in my bathroom right there in front of me as I got out of the shower. I used to love it before, but in the last months of my pregnancy, I wanted to turn that mirror around or remove it. Thus, I learned to get out of the shower in a speed mode all the while without glancing at myself.

The darkness in my room didn't help either. At first when I moved into Craig and Cyndie's home, I loved it. The basement felt nice with no window and no noise. It was wonderful to be in that place. I felt at peace when I was in the basement, which became my hiding cave. I could go in there, read my bible and pray to feel at peace or go in and cry when I was feeling sorry for myself. However, as my pregnancy continued, I grew bigger and as I gained weight, no matter how many people told me that I looked good, I never believed any of them. As people say the beauty comes from within, it's true when you are gloomy inside it doesn't matter how beautiful you are on the outside. the darkness inside is darker than the outer beauty; beside, no one can convince you how good you look if you don't feel it yourself.

As days went by, as much as I loved my hiding place, the room became my enemy. When I was there, I couldn't think anything positive anymore. I felt sad, which caused me to spend more time crying than praying. The darkness in my room matched my mood. Every time I entered, I became depressed. The last few months I no longer wanted to get out of my bed. Since I couldn't tell what time it was anyway, I would sleep until two in the afternoon. That's how dark my room was. This darkness helped me, because I didn't want to get up anyway. I didn't want to face the world.

There was a time I wished I had at least a little window in my room to show me that at least it was morning, regardless of the darkness in my heart. My last month (month nine, of course), I avoided my room as much time as possible. I spent time at my sister's house, or any other places because I didn't want to be in my room anymore. Inside my heart and spirit, I felt homeless even though I now had a home (what is a home if there is no peace of the mind in it?). There were days I wished I didn't have to see anyone, but I always had to drag myself out of bed so the people I lived with would not worry about me.

One thing that helped me was the gospel CD Hunter brought me from Rwanda. There were a couple of songs I loved on it. I listened to this CD every day while pregnant. When I was home, it was on and when in my car, the music was playing. I even took it to work several times when I was working alone. My last month of my pregnancy there was nothing I could do in order to calm my moods and sometimes this CD didn't work.

I kept myself busy with two classes, and by working three days a week until almost the end of my pregnancy. I decided not to sit at home and feel sorry for myself. Sometimes I felt all this busyness was not enough to stop me from thinking, even though I knew that I didn't have the energy to do anything else. My pregnancy felt like a never-ending journey and my energy and patience were running out. My job ended the beginning of May and then I finished school May 12th. My baby boy was born on May 25th. By the time I had him, I was emotionally and physically exhausted. In fact – by May 15th I was begging him to come out. Even though my doctor had told me that the baby's due date was May 29th and that he might come two weeks late, I couldn't imagine waiting two more weeks.

———

The day before I gave birth, I had a regular prenatal appointment at ten that morning. As I drove there, I was wondering how long it would take him to come out. I did not think I could go on for another two weeks. However, on my way to my scheduled appointment, I felt a gush of liquid coming out. I didn't think too much of it, thinking it was just discharge which is common during pregnancy.

When I arrived at the clinic, the nurse took me and did a routine urine sample. When I was going to pee in the cup she had given me, the gush I felt before, gushed out into the cup before I could even force myself to pee. I thought it was weird but didn't think too much of it. The liquid didn't look like urine at all. When the nurse saw it, she said, "Do you have a urinary tract infection. This pee is awfully cloudy." I told her not that I knew of. She weighed me, and I was happy that I weighed the same as the time of my last visit. I didn't want to gain any extra weight. I had already gained about thirty-five pounds.

After the nurse was done with everything, she sent me to the room where I would wait for the doctor to come and examine me. I waited there for a little while and then when the doctor came, he asked me how I was feeling. The doctor offered to scratch my membrane again so the baby could come faster. He had offered that to me during my previous visit, and he had told me that there was a 50/50 chance of getting contractions sooner. I refused the offer then because I didn't see the point of rushing this child after waiting nine months.

Even though the doctor explained to me that the chance of the baby getting an infection after the scratching of the membrane was low, I didn't want to risk anything that could harm my baby. I told him again that the baby would come when it was his time without me disturbing him. He went on to check me to see if my cervix had opened up yet. But as he did it, the same type of gush, which felt like the earlier one happened again. When he saw that he asked, "When did this start to come out?" I told him that I was in the car coming to the appointment. Dr. Thompson told me that he was going to check and see if it was what he thought it was. He told me that it looked like amniotic fluid, but he would go check to be sure.

After several minutes, when the doctor came back, he told me that my membrane had ripped, but my cervix was still closed. That explained why I had any contractions yet. I was told to go home and wait there. Then, he told me to meet him at the hospital at 5:00 p.m. and he would induce me. I left the clinic about eleven in the morning. On my way home, I called my sister to inform her of my doctor's instructions.

However, in the car I could feel that the liquid was coming often. My sister was at work. After I talked to her, I called Cyndie's number, but she was not there. I started to get anxious and wondered what if I started going into labor without anyone at home. I called my friend

Aline to see if at least I could meet her at home, but she was not at home, and didn't answer her cellphone either. I drove home and thought maybe Cyndie would be there by the time I got home. I got home, but as I pulled into the driveway, I felt my first contraction. I panicked because no one was there. I called my sister again. This time she told me to hang on, that she was coming, because either way she would not be able to concentrate knowing that I was about to have a baby.

It was now noon. The contractions were coming every eleven minutes. Around one that afternoon, my sister Christina arrived, but by the time she got there, the contractions were getting strong and painful, about every seven minutes. When I saw her pulling in the driveway, I ran to her car without wearing any shoes – never mind the bag I planned to take. Before another contraction came, I was racing. When she saw me, she just laughed. I told her that we needed to go and we didn't need the bag. Good thing she didn't pay much attention to me. After ignoring me, she went in and grabbed what I already had put in the suitcase.

Christina told me that it was too early to go to the hospital, because she knew for sure if we went, they would send us back home. We went to my sister's house since it was closer to the hospital. When we got to her house, the contractions increased, they were closer together and more painful than before. After an hour, they were coming every three minutes. Every time I had a contraction, I threw up. When I threw up, I felt the urge to push. Christina told me to try not to push, but I couldn't help it.

Even though I felt like I was going insane, my sister seemed calm. I didn't know if it was because she used to be a midwife or because he didn't want to freak me out. When I began throwing up, Christina rushed me to the hospital because she told me that she thought I was ready to have the baby. When we arrived at the hospital, they took us right in to see the nurse. She checked me and found out that I was at 5 cm. The nurse rushed and told me she was calling my doctor to come because he was supposed to have come at five. An hour later, the nurse returned and checked me again. She told me then I was 6-7 cm. She told me that if it continued as it was I might deliver the baby soon.

By this time, the contractions were so painful, and I was in such agony. The contractions were so close together that I hardly had a chance to catch my breath in between them. By then, my sister was cheering me on and telling me to hold on and to try hard because by five o'clock, the baby would be out. At five, they told me that I was about nine centimeters and that I should start to get ready to push because the baby was coming soon. No matter what any of them wanted or thought – I had run out of any energy to push. I was so tired I couldn't hold a glass of water. My whole body was shaking. An hour later, when the nurse came back to check me, she looked disappointed and told me that I was still at nine centimeters. After nine centimeters, my labor stopped. At six, it was the same, at seven, nothing changed, by eight, nothing.

At eight, I told my doctor that I couldn't take it anymore. Exhaustion, pain, puking my lungs out. I couldn't take it any longer. Since I hadn't eaten for two days, and I didn't have anything in my stomach. The last six hours I had been throwing up water, and when there was no water, only air came out. I told my doctor that I didn't care how he was going to do it, as long as he took that baby out. He could cut me open, I could care less. Finally, I had had enough – eight hours of pain was enough.

My original birth plan was to deliver naturally, without using medication. However, after all those hours of torture, I told my doctor that I took everything I had said back. I couldn't bare the pain any longer. He tried to explain to me the consequences of the medicine they would give me and how I was very close to having the baby. I told him that I didn't care anymore, just take the baby out or give me something to stop the pain. How could you reason with a mad pregnant woman who was in labor? After a while, he gave up. He told me that he would get the doctor who would give me the epidural. After ten minutes, I began to whine to the nurse telling her that nobody cared about my pain. Poor woman I sent her back and forth to see if the doctor was coming and what was taking him so long. I don't know if my doctor was stalling to see if I would have the baby while I waited or maybe he could not find an epidural specialist. An hour later, the epidural doctor came and gave me the medicine. After the medicine took affect, it felt like a miracle. I could breathe again.

———————

The past several hours my nieces and some of my friends had been waiting outside. When my nieces came in, I sent them away because I couldn't stand anyone in the room besides my sister. I couldn't even let my sister answer the phone. Even though I had promised them they could be in the room. After the epidural, they came in again. The mad woman that I was at the time vanished after the epidural. I talked and laughed with them like nothing had happened. For a moment, I was able to forget my current nightmare. However, everything comes with a price. After the epidural, my contractions became irregular and then I became stuck at nine-centimeters.

By midnight, the heartbeat of my son dropped. They gave me an oxygen mask to put on my mouth. At times, I was starting to fall asleep, but I couldn't sleep because I could still feel the little contractions in my back. They were so irritating. But it was nothing compared to what I experienced before the medicine. Around two o'clock in the morning, the doctor said that they would reduce the medication so I could push. When they reduced it, it was so painful I was unable to push. I had horrible back contractions disabling me to push. This time I was still on the oxygen, because my baby's heart rate hadn't gotten any better. I guess he was tired as well and stubborn to come out. He didn't want to cooperate at all.

By three in the morning, they told me that I had to push because the baby was ready. I felt that I couldn't do as they asked. Christina was stern with me, telling me that I had to push and stop being a wimp. But all what I wanted was to just fall asleep and forget everything. The pain was still in my back, and I couldn't sleep. It was excruciating pain. By four in the morning, I felt that I had had enough, I wanted to give birth.

Since I couldn't tell when the contractions were happening, I told them to tell me when they were occurring so I could push. By five, I really wanted him born. I pushed, taking breaks in between, which drove my sister crazy. She told me that I was being selfish because the baby needed to be out. By six, I felt that I would do all in my power to get him out. I pushed and pushed then at 6:51 a.m. on May 25th Alexander was born. When they pulled him out of me, it was the most overwhelming feeling I have ever felt in my life. At that instant, I forgot how painful it had been throughout the process and what all I had been going through the last eighteen hours.

I was so exhausted, and when they put him on my stomach, I didn't even recognize that he didn't cry. After a couple of minutes, I realized that there were a lot of people over him. I kept asking Christina if my baby was okay. She did not give me a real answer. She answered me but without telling me what's really going on. She kept telling me that everything would be okay; I nodded and didn't worry much because I was physically drained.

Cyndie and one of my nieces, Gabby, had been there all night. Gabby told me that the baby was healthy. I couldn't believe how brave Gabby was. She had been by my side all night and when the baby was born, Gabby cut the umbilical cord. I couldn't believe her, a sixteen-year-old girl being so loving and brave.

Some time passed and I began to be nervous to see my baby. I had asked Gabby how the baby was, and she told me for the third time that the baby was okay. Finally, I heard a baby cry then I realized Alexander didn't make a sound when he came out. However, later they told me that when Alexander was born – he was blue and had not been breathing. Christina had put her hand on him and prayed for him when she saw that there were no signs of life. She had called my pastor to pray for the baby. Christina had told me that she was so scared that she didn't know what she would have told me if anything bad had happened to him.

When Alexander was born, he was the most beautiful baby I had ever seen, and he looked so much like his father. He really looked like a mini-me of him. So much for what I had hoped for when I was pregnant! In the hospital, my nurse told me, "I have to admit that you have the most beautiful baby." She told me that all the nurses took a vote on all the babies in the hospital at the time and thought that Alexander was the most beautiful baby there.

When I look at him, I say to myself that he really is worth every bit of every pain and all the suffering I went through. When I was pregnant, I focused on how fat and ugly I was, and I prayed to God to please give me a beautiful baby to console me (I know that's a vanity prayer but it's what I truly prayed for). He really answered my prayers, and I am grateful for that. When I look at him, I tell myself that he really is a gift from above; because I couldn't have ended up with a child like Alexander if it hadn't been for God. My nieces teased me, "How can you have such a beautiful baby? We knew you could have a beautiful baby, but not this beautiful." I fought with them, but deep down I felt the same way. Aurore my niece still thinks I have the children she was supposed to have.

Chapter 30

"For God so loved the world that he gave his one and only son, that whoever believes in him shall not perish but have eternal life"

~ *John 3:16*

After Alexander was born, we had a revival at church and a visiting pastor from Las Vegas preached that God is able to take the situation that caused you pain, suffering and shame and turn that into beauty. He is capable of picking you out of the ash pile of sin and making something completely beautiful out of you. This infuriated the devil. The pastor used the analogy of beauty from ashes. This was comforting and reassuring knowing God's promise is bigger than my failure, my sin, my weaknesses, and anything life will throw in my path. God turned my mistake and shortcomings into blessings. I believe there is nothing that could make the devil more enraged than having a beautiful boy God blessed me with to show me that He still loved me and there is nothing I could ever do to change that. I thought that the message the pastor shared with us was mine. It spoke to my heart.

Through my son, I have experienced a love of God I never experienced in my life before. It gives me a warm feeling when I think that God loves me beyond the love I have for my son. Alexander had such a wonderful spirit, and when he smiled at me in the morning, I just wanted to melt away. He just makes my heart sing. Everyone loved my infant son when he was born - little children, middle-aged friends and family, the elderly. When I was at church or home, I never knew where he was. He went from the hands of one person to the other. There were times in the past that I gave up asking where he was – I would just see my son when he wanted to be nursed. After surviving such a hard birth, I thought it was a blessing to share him.

After Alexander's birth, we both went to live with my sister Christina. If people wanted to come to visit my son and I – it was easier for them to come to my sister's home. We moved because I felt that I didn't want to freak out these poor people I was living with. When there is a newborn, Rwandan people (friends, family, neighbors, even strangers, who heard about the baby) come unannounced night or day and bringing food – presents for the baby and the new mom. I thought this would be too much for my friends. Although I loved and still love this part of our culture, I did not want to drive these godly people crazy.

Christina took several days off so she could be with me. All those days she was home, the only thing I did was take a bath, nurse, eat and sleep. When my child was crying, someone else was holding him. When he needed to be bathed, someone took care of it. I never did anything for a month. After that, when my sister went back to work, my nieces Carine, Gabby and Aurore took over and bossed me around like no tomorrow. If they came back from school and I hadn't eaten, they were about to kill me.

My nieces were more brutal than their mother, especially Carine. Carine yelled at me to eat so I could produce milk for the baby. That was their main concern and it was because they loved their cousin. Actually, they called him their nephew. My nieces couldn't take their hands-off Alexander. They made me breakfast and lunch before they left for school. If they had a place to go after school, my nieces made sure to come home first before they went, and see if I was all set.

Through all this, Carine (the oldest), gave up her room to us and she was sleeping on the couch or sometimes in the room with her other

219

two sisters. All my nieces were so happy. They could have cared less if all of them had to give up all their rooms, as long Alexander was there. They used to tell me that they would be sad if I moved back to my place. They told me that I should stay with them and never go back. Even though we all knew that it would be hard to stay like that. Eventually, we all had to go back to our own lives.

Alexander was a special child, and I couldn't believe how he has had such an effect on people. My nieces had a neighbor Jeanette who lives with her triplet sister Jennifer, their younger sister Samantha and their grandmother. Jeanette and her triplet were about my age and Samantha was about my nieces' age. Jeanette had also been in a psychology class with me when I was pregnant. When I was pregnant, my feet would swell up to the point I couldn't find any shoes to fit me. I had to wear wide flip-flops all the time. I always wore pants that covered my feet. Jeannette never noticed that my feet were like that. Once, when we were in class, I told her that my feet were so big, and she was like – "Let me see!!" She was so excited, and I told her that I would show her, but she had to promise not to laugh. When I showed Jeannette my feet, she burst out the biggest laugh and laughed for about five minutes nonstop. From then on, I would see her from time to time trying to look at my feet again and doing it with one eye, so I would not catch her. If she was not looking at my feet she was playing with my belly telling Alexander to kick me. She talked to him asking him when he was coming out so she could play.

When Jeannette learned that I had come to live with my sister, she and her sisters came over. At that moment they, too, fell in love with Alexander. The younger sister could not eat breakfast or go to bed in the night without seeing him. She even cried when she had to go to New York to spend a summer vacation with her dad. Because she was not going to see Xander (that's what they called him) for the rest of summer vacation and Samantha was afraid that by the time she came back she would have missed a lot. Alexander was, and still is, a blessing to everyone. Whenever entering the parking lot, kids would come running up to see him, asking me if I was the mother of the beautiful baby, and asking if it was okay to let them come to my house to see him sometimes.

I stayed at my sister's for a little over two months. After I felt that my emotions were stable and I was strong enough to take care of myself and the baby, I determined I needed to go back to my own place. My sister Christina and my nieces needed to get back to their normal lives as well; and I needed to go face my reality of being a single mom. When I told Jeanette that I was moving back, she said, "Alexander is not only yours. He's for everybody, and you can't do that to us." Her triplet sister Jennifer told me that I was mean to hurt them like that and she asked why I couldn't continue sharing the love. They told me that besides their younger sister Samantha was not back yet from New York and she would not be happy.

The first week I went back to visit my sister after I moved back, Jeanette gave me the evil look and just said *hello* to Alexander without saying hello to me, telling him that I was mean to take him away from her.

The day I moved back it was distressing. Carine said, "This is so depressing I wish I was not here." I didn't want to leave either; leaving all these people who surrounded my son and I with love terrified me. I didn't want to face my unknown future with a child I have no clue how to take care of and raise. As much as I hated to go back to live in the basement in that dark room I spent most of the time crying, I felt that I needed to return to my normal life. Besides, Carine needed her room and my son needed an identity. I felt that I needed to start being his mother instead of enjoying being babied myself. It was about time I took on my own responsibility. It would have been nice if we had had a big house so each person could have their own privacy. But it was not like that. So, I had to return to my home no matter how much it caused me to scream inside. That day I was so emotional, but I promised myself not to cry.

All day I was on edge. I felt that if someone told me anything I would have cried. At the last minute, I packed around eight in the night. I thought that it would be late enough and less people would notice me leaving. When finished, I kind of rushed out so my sister would not tell me something that could make me break down. When I got in the car, I was with Carine and Aurore. I cried the minute I entered the car and all the way home, almost. Carine and Aurore were telling me not to cry. They were saying that things would be better, and even though I was moving back, it didn't mean we would not see each other again. They told me that they would come visit me. How embarrassing that felt at the time.

It is not that I have anything against the family I lived with - Craig and Cyndie are the most wonderful people I know. If all people were more like them, this world would be a better place. Craig and Cyndie welcomed me in their home and have been there for me since day one. To tell you the truth, I see them as my family. When I was in labor, Cyndie was at my side all night without her daughter, who was one year old and still nursing. She left her little child the whole night to be with me. When I was pregnant, she made me breakfast every morning. Who can you compare these people to? They are a gift from God.

Regardless of how I feel about Cyndie and Craig; moving from my sister's back to their house, I felt that if I went back and lived in that room I hated in the last term of my pregnancy, I would have a nervous breakdown. I didn't want to be like that since I was now with my son. I was praying that God would have to make me stronger. The transition of moving from Christina's place to Craig and Cyndie's went well. However, some days were better than others. What helped me the most was that I felt God there, and I lived with people who loved me and prayed for me every day. What more could I have asked for?

———

When Alexander was born, I sent Hunter a message telling him that his son, Alexander had been born, so he would not hear it from someone else. On the second day I was in the hospital, he sent me flowers and chocolates and a little note telling me *thanks* and *congratulations*. Receiving something from him surprised me. After these gifts, he never called, all the time I was in hospital.

Then a couple weeks after I took home Alexander from the hospital, Hunter sent me an email thanking me for having a cute boy, asking me how the baby was, and wanting to know if I could send him some more pictures of Alexander. He told me that he would come to see him soon. When I saw this email, I thought, *maybe he's had a change of heart*. Who knew; a baby could bring a miracle. I answered Hunter's email and told him that the baby was good. I told him that he was more than welcome to come see him, and hopefully, soon. Between these emails, my son's father asked me if he could add a name to what I had named Alexander. I was hesitating but I thought about it and felt adding a name to Alexander would not kill me; plus, if that would get him closer to his son – *let it be*. After this email, I didn't hear from Hunter for few weeks. Then later, I got another email asking me how the baby was and how come I didn't send him the pictures he had requested.

When I saw this email, I didn't want to respond to him because he hadn't even mentioned why he had never come to visit and see his son for the first time ever. At least he should have given me some excuse as to why he never showed up. I didn't want to give Hunter a photograph that he could be showing off when he didn't even care enough about this child to visit us yet. I didn't want to play games with him anymore. I really wanted to know what he wanted in my son's life and if he was not going to be there, I didn't want to play these mind games of his anymore. Each day I had been praying, asking God to just please give me a sign showing me that if Hunter had changed and cared about his son. It seemed to me if this happened then I could go on with my life.

I was mentally exhausted. I went through a range of emotions, thinking what if Hunter never came in my child's life? *What if later I got married again and the husband did not like my son? Would my son be sad? What if my son didn't like him? Then he would be miserable.* I went through all these what if's and other what if's. I always hoped and wished he could change and come take us away and we would be a family again. I don't know why as women we torture ourselves with all these questions, which we cannot answer or find solutions for. Only God can change the heart of a man, not us! No matter how much we obsess over it, or how much we beg or lower ourselves to the ground or wish and pray so much to cause something to change for us. It is not us. Only God can change the heat of a man, period. I knew what kind of man Hunter was but I was afraid to accept it.

When Alexander was very young I thought many times that I would never get involved with any other guy. Still, I was miserable. I was still in my twenties so I thought there was no way I would be single for the rest of my life. Not that I was thinking to be involved with anyone soon; because men were on the bottom of my list. But I knew it would not be like that forever. I hoped and prayed that maybe if Hunter would change and be the father of my child as he was supposed to, that would make all of us happy. I had all this wishful thinking that became obsessions that dictated how I lived. This obsession has so much of a stronghold on my life. Even if God would have brought someone in my life, I would not have seen him because I was a prisoner of Hunter's rejection and of my own fear. Instead of working so hard to move on and let God heal me, I spent so much time dreaming and obsessing about when Hunter might come back. How pathetic!

After this email about the pictures came, I decided to write an email to Hunter and ask him what he really wanted.

I told him that what happened in the past was over, and the baby was here. Regardless of how we felt about each other, that we should overlook that and get along for the sake of our son. I told Hunter that I could see now that he seemed somewhat interested, but I wanted to know what his future plans were and any intentions he had for the baby. Also, I told him I wanted him to be in our son's life 100%, and I didn't want him to make promises he would never fulfill. And if he thought that he could not be able to do that, he should leave us alone.

Also, I wrote that I needed to file for a divorce, but because we had a minor child, it would be easier for both of us to do a joint divorce, which include parenting plan petitions. I gave him the website of the state to go see the information himself. I also told him that as long as we were still married, I couldn't sign anything for my son without his signature as well; which would be so much pain for me. I gave him the date I planned to file divorce papers and thought it would provide him time to think it over and time to plan a visit if he wanted to reconcile the relationship.

Hunter replied the next day, telling me that my email was a good idea because he was thinking the same thing, as well. But, he told me in order to reply to all the questions I asked him, I would need to explain what I meant by my statement about him 'being in Alexander's life 100%'. So, I told Hunter what I meant by that was just to do what he said he would do, because I didn't want him to hurt my son. I told him regardless of what I thought of him; he was still the father of our son.

I told Hunter that even though Alexander was still too young to understand what was happening, it would not take too long for him to know who Hunter was and he also might have high expectations of his father. I also told him that I didn't want empty promises in my child's life like the ones he used to give me.

A couple of days later, Hunter replied. He told me how I was the one to blame for everything that had happened; how I should feel guilty for what I had done to him. He went on saying that what happened to me, I deserved. I had brought all of it upon myself.

After that email, I thought to myself *Poor thing; I am the one who left him when he was pregnant and broke all the plans we had.* How typical. In the whole email there was not even one thing telling me how he would be involved in his child's life, except that he would do what he could. He began the email telling me that he was going to tell me things that might hurt me and things he hadn't wanted to tell me when I was pregnant with his child. Wow, how caring he had been!

What he didn't know was that there was nothing in the email that was new to me. There was nothing in there that he had not already told me before leaving me. To me that email was no more hurtful than the things he had already said to me and the pain that has caused. Honestly, his words didn't hurt me even a little bit. Hunter's rejection was the answer to my prayer. It answered all the questions that had been going on in my head.

When I saw his email, it made me realize that he hadn't changed. He was still the same way he was when he left. I have to give Hunter credit though – he was very consistent. And when it comes to himself and his own needs, he had no shame. He went on telling me how if I divorced him, he would only see Alexander for two years. After that, he would have to find another place to go, and he marked that particular paragraph as the most important part of the email. It was as though he had been coming to see him every day since Alexander was born, and now I was taking this away from him. He also told me that in September he would start school full time. However, in another paragraph Hunter claimed he would do anything he could for the child.

In the end, he told me to take care of that baby. Like as if I was the nanny instead of Alexander's mother, or as if I hadn't already been taking care of him since he left. The email said he would come in a week and would call me the next day to confirm. After that, two months passed and I didn't hear from Hunter. Something clicked in me and I decided 'enough is enough' - that was it. I had waited for his call long enough. It never came and the deadline I gave him to come to sign the divorce papers had passed. After that, I went ahead and filed the divorce papers.

Chapter 31

"Don't let anyone look down on you because you are young, but set an example for the believers in speech, in conduct, in love, in faith, and in purity."

~ *1 Timothy 4:12*

I had filled out both joint and single petitions for divorce, because I knew that either might happen. It was rare when Hunter did what he said he would do, unless it was in his interest. The only thing I knew was that it was taking courage for me to fill out those papers and signing a check for the fee, I felt that he no longer was holding me back and that in all actuality, he had no *real* power over me. I felt that if Hunter ever changed his mind and came to meet/see his child, he would be more than welcome. If he didn't, it was not going to bother me either. Because of this final email – my heart and mind had found a place where I was happy and determined to raise my son alone with God, my family and friends.

————

Alexander is a blessing in my life, regardless of what we have been through and those things that might happen in our future. When I look at my dear son, I never regret anything. Actually, I would go through the circumstances all over again if I knew the outcome would bring this little boy into my life. I may not be the best mother in the eyes of others, but I know I will be the best mother in my son's eyes. I will raise him to be a man of integrity with God on my side. I love my son more than life itself. I pray that God will deliver Hunter from all the darkness he lives in and heal his heart. Because I believe in my heart that someday he will overcome the lie of the devil and accept the love of God, and live according to His plans.

Jesus has healed my wounds and has given me happiness in what I have. I came to accept and realized that I am a single mother who has been blessed by God. I will never teach my son to hate his father but to love him and pray for him. Maybe someday Hunter will come around, then Alexander would be able to enjoy his father and his father could know his son. If not, there is nothing else I can do except to keep reminding my son to realize and appreciate the Father of all fathers he has in his life. Who is better than Jesus Christ?

At this point, I am not sad that Hunter decided to have a life without us. What breaks my heart is the fact that he doesn't even show interest in his child. I just feel sorry for him. What he doesn't realize is that the King of Lies he choose to be attentive to chews people and spits them up. Hopefully, sooner than later, Hunter will recognize that. It is never too late to be welcomed by God in His hands. The truth is it takes some of us longer than others to realize that Satan is stealing joy from us, which God has given us freely. I truly don't despise him. I have forgiven him and I hope he will forgive himself and live freely with his life.

I know that I will make many mistakes along the way. However, I am not afraid or filled with shame anymore. I know Jesus paid the price for me; therefore, I will not live into sin or be a slave to sin. I have been set free and God has filled my life with such a peace that I can never explain to anyone. When the devil tries to lie to me, I bind him in Jesus' name because I know he has no single power over me. I am also not naïve. Yes, the single mother life is filled with difficulties. I welcome all those difficulties with God on my side and will not be bound by the fear of my future when I don't even know what's going to happen tomorrow. Instead, I believe through all those trials; I have assurance from heaven that Jesus will give me strength to face them all.

Some authors end their stories with, "Fin". For me, I say, "Commencement". The genocide caused me to lose motivation in life. The day my son Alexander was born, I wanted to live again for the first time in a long time. Before my son was born, it was very hard to see the reason to work hard or do anything that would bring success in my life because I didn't see the purpose. Now, I have a reason to live. My son, Alexander, is someone who will say, *This is my mom*, the powerful three letter word. I am so excited for this adventurous journey we call life I am traveling with my son. This is the commencement of my life after such a long hopeless life, I have been restored by the Grace of God. " Therefore, I have hope: because of the Lord's great love we are not consumed, for his compassions never fail. They are new every morning; great is your faithfulness" Lamentation 3:21-23. The Omniscient God holds our future.

PART V: Healing

Epilogue

"Surely, he took up our pain and bore our suffering,

yet we considered him punished by God,

stricken by him, and afflicted.

But he was pierced for our transgressions,

he was crushed for our iniquities;

the punishment that brought us peace was on him,

and by his wounds we are healed."

Isaiah 53:4-5

It's been over ten years since my oldest son Alexander was born and I am still fighting. However, I can confidently say that God has never given up on me, no matter how much I have disappointed Him. I wish I could tell you that I have lived a pure life (as I proclaimed at the end of the last chapter of this book ten years ago when I first began writing it) but, I am humiliated to say that I have many times broken my Lord's heart.

Even though I have been a rotten sinner, He has always reminded me that his holiness and his righteousness illuminate my sinful life.

About seven years ago, one Sunday morning, I could feel the spirit of the devil on me as I was about to enter the church. This feeling was bombarding me and filling my mind with doubt and condemnation asking why I was even bothering to going to church. In the midst of that, I heard a calm, small voice saying, "You may not be holy, but I am Holy." This lifted me up so much and reminded me that it's not my righteousness that draws me to God but by His Son's righteousness and His grace alone.

The story of Alexander's father and I didn't end when Hunter left me. I continued to chase him and even managed to convince myself that moving closer to him would benefit my son. Despite the fact that even before Alexander was born, he never showed interest in being a father and had never wanted to be a constant in his life. When he started coming to see him, he came as part of our divorce settlement. From that point, the time became longer between visits: four months, six months, a year, or however long his conscience could hold him at bay. Or however long he could stand people asking him how his son was doing.

Nevertheless, for some odd reason after I finished my graduate program I decided to move closer to where Hunter lived. You see, I found myself believing his excuse that the reason he was not completely involved with his son was that he lived too far away. So, I convinced myself that if I got a job near where Hunter lived, it would be a sign that God wanted me to move closer to him. Oh! The lies we tell ourselves! First of all, if God has removed Hunter from my life why would God tell me to follow him? Sometimes we want something so bad even when deep down we know it is wrong for us, we convince ourselves it's God when in reality it is our emotions and devil doing the work!

Along the way, he and my sinful desire charmed me as well; many times, I put him first before God. Then, he would disappear and return to not caring at all. My life would then be filled with sorrow and shame. Though, God being a faithful God, He would lift me up again. Every time God lifted me up and filled me with His presence I always said *never again will I sacrifice His love*. However, when Alexander's dad gave me a little attention or interest I dropped everything and put the man on a pedestal. And then Hunter – the man of course - would drop me like hot potatoes. It became a vicious cycle.

You see, even though God was always there for me, I was so blinded by my sins and never saw it that way. I just treated Him secondary. Still with all my sinful heart, God showed me with His love and blessings, and then I became a spoiled brat. When I prayed, He answered me right away, because He promised to never leave us alone. When I didn't get what I wanted, I started throwing a tantrum like a two-year-old. All my life has been like a rollercoaster; one day in love with God and then on another day, I would find myself feeling sorry for myself; holding hands with Lucifer as I allowed him to whisper his lies into my mind.

It always astonishes me how easily I can abandon God's path and believe the lies of Satan when he promises nothing but misery. The devil paints this illusion of pleasure and for some strange reason, I crave that even though I know that, in the end, the stakes are high. No matter how many times I told myself that I would never end up in those situations again, I still never seemed to learn the lesson I needed for complete freedom from Hunter.

Our God is longsuffering and His mercy never ends. He waited for me and when needed, He put balm on my wounds and tended to my hurt and I felt restored. Lacking restraint, I would run to the devil again and again. That has been the dance all my life; until my King said, "Enough is enough. I can't let you keep destroying yourself." He drew me closer to him and played a movie of my life. Then and there, I surrendered and let him take the charge. I knew if I continued to do what I was doing, I would be heading on the road to hell. Now my desire was to pull myself toward Jesus instead of being pulled in by the opposite of what God wanted for me. Through Him I am promised protection, eternal life, forgiveness, and blessings; and these blessings continue from me, to my children and their children…still, to this day and for all eternity. What is better than that? Besides, the many times the devil dropped me and I fell into the mess of sin, who was there to hold me but Jesus Jehovah Rapha?

I danced with the devil and played Christian for so long until Jesus said enough is enough. I needed tough love as they say, since I needed serious discipline and God needed full attention from me. First, God took the job that He had given me and kept me jobless for years. I lost this job when I was hundreds of miles away from my family and friends. He completely closed all the doors. Nevertheless, instead of seeing this as an opportunity to get right with my Savior, I took the easy way out and lived however I wanted. Satan has a way of blinding us and causing us to see and hear what we want to hear. During the years I was jobless, I wrestled with my sin and God. For months I would continue with praying and feeling good about myself and then other months my sin would kick in and I would wallow in feeling no hope and no faith and became angry at God.

———— ——

God kept pursuing and I was very stubborn to surrender to Him. One rainy morning, I was driving to Health and Human Services to see if they could help me pay my utility bills and when I got there I was looked down upon, which caused me to feel low and humiliated. Then, I looked all around myself and saw all the people who were in pain and suffering, I looked at myself and hated myself for being in that same position. I was thinking *How did I get here*? I had a master's degree and thousands of dollars' worth of school loans to prove it but I could not provide for my family or myself. When I got outside, it was pouring down rain and I was crying to God with tears streaming on my face, screaming inside at God, "God, how can you put me in this position? God, you gave me an education, helped me to finish when some days I was ready to drop out; and still, you helped me keep going. Was my

233

education for nothing?" I told Him, *At least I would treat these people better if I had opportunity to work there.*

I sat in my car and kept weeping for myself and all those people who were at the health and human services seeking help. Also, I cried to God and asked Him why He could not help me and asked what does He want from me. Then in a little small still voice, I heard, "I want your heart, give it to me," My heart! My broken heart, my shattered heart, or my rotten heart? I didn't see why He wanted my heart at all.

All in the same prayer, I mumbled that He could have my heart but deep down I knew that I was lying to myself because even myself I was not convinced of my own real answer. Once again, I silenced that voice and kept going with my careless life. If I was smart and obedient, I would have woken up and begged my Savior to take it and He would have given me another one that's pure and holy like His. The word of God says, "Do not grieve the Holy Spirit of God whom you were sealed by the day of redemption" (Ephesians 4:30). All my life, that's what I had done. I grieved the Holy Spirit. All my life I had treated God as a last solution; or as a genie in a bottle that could be rubbed, and a miracle would happen. When things were good, I put Him on shelf. When things were bad, I fetched Him. Being a wonderful God, He always blessed me no matter which way I had sought Him – the fact was that at least I sought Him. That is all He requires for His love to be given and/or shown. When I was young and sinned and got hurt, God didn't condemn me but healed my wounds and protected me. Instead of putting Him first, I took Him for granted.

Instead of taking this time of unemployment as a turning point for my relationship with God and letting God teach me, I became angry and bitter toward God and did not see the point of serving Him. I saw Him as a God who loves, blesses or curses whoever he wants. This belief caused me to feel as though I was cursed. Therefore, I didn't see the point of serving Him any longer. Sinful thoughts with no fear crept in and I began watching movies I had no business watching, with filthy language and being okay with it. You have to know me to understand what I am talking about – to see how this behavior just really wasn't the real me. Now, I don't know what it is but there is something that sickens me to my stomach when I hear cursing in the movies or somewhere else. So, when this time I watched movies like this and was okay with it, I knew my soul might have slipped a bit.

For the first time in seven years, since my son was born, I had begun losing interest in attending church and church usually was something that kept me going. However, I hadn't stop going to church because I didn't want my son and niece Carine we were living at the time to question me. But when I was there my heart felt as though it was somewhere else. Before now, there had never been anything I loved more than being in the church. That's where I felt most at peace. Most of the time, I wished the sermon and the singing at church didn't end. Mostly, I wished I could stay longer and never go outside to face the realities of life.

Then, for the first time in my life, I slept with my son's father without feeling guilt-ridden and ashamed of it. As embarrassing as it is to admit, I truly had done something to defy God. This was not the first time I had sinned with Hunter but it was the first time I sinned as an act to defy God. After that I felt a darkness overshadowing my life that I never thought existed. I became cold and indifferent toward God in my heart, but, still, I didn't care. The overshadowing peace and joy of God that had covered me all my life left, never felt like this in my life. It was the scariest time. I lived with a taunting fear; I lived in agony, in the dark. Sleep became difficult for me and I lived in constant torture. I felt so far from God and I wished I could die. I can't count how many times I laid beneath my bed begging God to please take my life. If I didn't have fear of leaving Alexander or fear about where I would end up, I would have carried through with killing myself.

Throughout that time of wrestling with God and my sin, I sought some semblance of comfort in my son's father. However, it was an illusion since we both knew there was no love in it. I was humiliated by my own behavior and I hated myself for it and I despised what I had become. This time, there was no presence of God in my life. I lived in the dark and my spirit was tormented by my sins. Two months into my agony, I received a card from my friend Lisa with two hundred dollars in it and a wonderful message that quoted Isaiah 41: *"But you, O Israel, my servant, Jacob, whom I have chosen, you descendants of Abraham my friend, I took you from the ends of the earth, from its farthest corners I called you. I said, 'You are my servant'; I have chosen you and have not rejected you. So do not fear, for I am with you; do not be dismayed, for I am your God. I will strengthen you and help you; I will uphold you with my righteous right hand."*

After I read this card, something broke in my heart. I couldn't believe that God could still love me after defying him. There, He showed me that He doesn't love me because I act good or live a sinless life. He loves me because He *is* love; regardless of my shortcomings and there is nothing I could ever do to change how much He loves me; *what undeserving love!*

I broke down, cried, then bent down and repented. But the presence of God didn't instantly arrive – perhaps I was still being disciplined. My thoughts were that I deserved every bit of the silent treatment I received and even told God that. In my heart, I was horrified. I cried to God to renew his Spirit in me but my cries seemed to be all in vain. I lived in fear and at the same time, told God that instead of living without His presence, I was better off if He could kill me. Still, there was a silence.

The nightmare of not having the comfort of my God's presence was not my only misery. My friend's card that snapped me from the hands of the devil came a little late. There was a price to pay for the great sin that I had committed. The discipline was still going on; unfortunately. That month I missed my period. Afterward, I became mortified and began living in denial. *There is no way I could be pregnant...* the second month came and still my period did not happen. My denial continued. At the time, I didn't even want to take the pregnancy test to make sure. I told myself that if I waited longer it would go away. I started feeling strange, craving things I had never eaten before, and then the nausea kicked in.

I decided to tell Alexander's father about what I was feeling and he assured me not to worry. He said, "There's no way you could be pregnant." Hunter continued, "It's not like there is anything else we can do." (This time he didn't dare tell me to abort the child but that was his hint). Then, He added, "Are you sure it's mine?" I laughed inside. Deja vu! The true colors of the Hunter I knew! I didn't even justify or try to defend myself. Instead, I just shook my head and got up and told him, "You know what... the first time I had a child with you I didn't know what to do but now I do. Don't worry about anything, we will be okay." That was the last time willingly I spoke to Hunter face-to-face and it has been almost six years.

Thus, I hoped that I was not pregnant but the fear and the signs stayed with me. Then I decided to go to the clinic nearby where I lived that offered free pregnancy tests. There, my nightmare was confirmed.

I couldn't believe I was going back to where I had been seven years earlier. Having another baby with the same man who doesn't care about me, or even care about his first child – was depressing, at best. What did I do to myself and my kids? This time I was ashamed of myself, I felt a wall between me and God. *Will God ever forgive me? Will I ever be able to bend my knees and pray to my savior and feel His closeness?*

Quite possibly, I never knew the definition of shame until then. Nearly seven years later, I was back where I was in 2006. This time I was pregnant with my second child and I was alone again but it felt different. I didn't cry because Alexander's father broke my heart the second time, there was no *real* heart to break in the first place. Being transparent and honest to myself, Hunter never promised me anything this time. When I moved closer to him in the name of my son's benefits, he had his own place and I had mine; all these rendezvous we had together against my God and behind my son and my family's back was my own doing. *I the daughter of the Most High God who chose to become a*

237

booty call. I had brought myself into this mess this time. I knew better. This time I was ashamed and grieved about breaking my Savior's heart. God made sure and showed me that all my life I have compromised Him. I was heartbroken because it took me seven years and another child to realize that God is the one who blessed me, held my hands when my sin put me under. He blessed me and still I never put Him first. All these years, I put a man first above my King. This grieved me beyond physical pain. Never had I known such pain, emotional, mental, spiritual and all this led to even a physical pain, causing me to know my strongest need was to put my King – my God – first in my life even if it meant losing Hunter or any other man for that matter. Even if I found a man who was right for me and we lived happily ever after – I now knew my God had to come first.

I realized that prior to this pregnancy, I never really repented and grieved by my sin until I felt total forgiveness of my Savior in the midst of my soiled life. Oswald Chambers in *My Utmost for His Highest* wrote beautifully: *Conviction of sin is one of the most uncommon things that ever happens to a person. It is the beginning of an understanding of God. Jesus Christ said that when the Holy Spirit came He would convict people of sin (see John 16:8). And when the Holy Spirit stirs a person's conscience and brings him into the presence of God, it is not that person's relationship with others that bothers him but his relationship with God— "Against You, You only, have I sinned, and done this evil in your sight . . ." (Psalm 51:4). The wonders of conviction of sin, forgiveness, and holiness are so interwoven that it is only the forgiven person who is truly holy. He proves he is forgiven by being the opposite of what he was previously, by the grace of God. Repentance always brings a person to the point of saying, "I have sinned." The surest sign that God is at work in his life is when he says that and means it. Anything less is simply sorrow for having made foolish mistakes— a reflex action caused by self-disgust.*

The entrance into the kingdom of God is through the sharp, sudden pains of repentance colliding with man's respectable "goodness." Then the Holy Spirit, who produces these struggles, begins the formation of the Son of God in the person's life (see Galatians 4:19). This new life will reveal itself in conscious repentance followed by unconscious holiness, never the other way around. The foundation of Christianity is repentance. Strictly speaking, a person cannot repent when he chooses— repentance is a gift of God. The old Puritans used to pray for "the gift of tears." If you ever cease to understand the value of repentance, you allow yourself to remain in sin. Examine yourself to see if you have forgotten how to be truly repentant. Oswald Chambers could not cut it to the heart with even more clarity. This is what I felt when I was pregnant with my second son Azariah.

God showed me the rebellion didn't start when I started sinning, it started when I gave my life to Christ many years ago with the Kenyan women. He reminded me that that day I gave Him some of my pain and didn't surrender to him all the ugly pain. He laid upon my heart: *Sure, you forgave the people who killed your family but you didn't give me the self-hate and the heinous crime they committed against your body. Alternatively, you grew up to fill that void and pain with men, and instead of trusting me enough to take all away and heal you wholeheartedly.*

I remembered how I thought there was no way God could take the ugliness I felt inside of me. All the years after genocide, I constantly lived in hidden self-loathing that I couldn't see how someone could love me. There, I repented and I gave it to my Savior. I gave Him the ugly, the pain, the fear, the anger, the hate, bitterness the loneliness and then I was free from the chains of the enemy. The black dark secret memories washed away. – pure as the white snow.

————

When I was pregnant with Azariah, I realized that I never truly repented because if I did I would not have gone back and forth picking up what my Savior had erased in my life. I believe even the guilt I felt – that guilt was the self-disgust of my behavior, not true repentance. When my desire drove me to rebel against what my family and culture have taught me; I got disgusted with myself but was not moved to be grieved by my sins.

This time it was different; I was tormented by my sin. I was surrounded by deep dark cloud. My heart was pressed and I couldn't breathe properly for weeks. I cried to God, He seemed far away and for once, I was thankful that He didn't reply and come to my rescue. The more days I felt pain, the more I thanked Him for disciplining me. I told Him that I deserved the silence and the tormenting spirit. Evidently, I needed to feel the pain so I could experience the pain I had caused Him. I had taken so much for granted His kind love and forgiveness. I remembered while I was pregnant with Alexander, I was grieved by the pain his father had caused me and wondered if I would ever be able to laugh again because I was so heartbroken. However, this time, it was a pain deep in my heart and the agony of my sin, I couldn't believe how far I have fallen and how much I have grieved my savior. For two months, I was so deeply consumed with God's silence. For the first time, I felt and imagined how it must feel to be in hell.

I cried to God day and night. He was silent but, on the December 7th of 2012 after my son went to school, I sat and cried to God. While praying, I asked Him to please take away the tormenting spirit and I told Him that instead of living as if His presence was no longer with me that He should take my life. As I have done so many nights and days; I was sobbing and crying to him and completely broken with total surrender in my heart and mind. I was listening to this beautiful song by Plum: BEAUTIFUL HISTORY

I have made mistakes and I have been afraid

I have felt alone then You called my name

Things were crashing loudly, happening all around me

But Your still small voice was all that I could hear

I am here, I'm holding you

You'll make it through this, I am here, I am here

I am here, I'm holding you

You'll make it through this, I am here, I am here

Whenever you run away

Whenever you lose your faith

It's just another stroke of the pen on the page

A lonely ray of hope is all that you'll need to see a beautiful history

Well, I've been such a fool when I've known the truth

I've wasted so much time doing what I wanted to

I've been living solely for myself and myself only

But Your still small voice is whispering

Whenever you run away

Whenever you lose your faith

It's just another stroke of the pen on the page

A lonely ray of hope is all that you'll need to see a beautiful history

I toss and turn and scream, I try to do everything

With two feet on the ground I just keep falling down again

I feel so far from home, completely all alone

And then I hear You say I am here, I am here

Whenever you run away

Whenever you lose your faith

It's just another stroke of the pen on the page

A lonely ray of hope is all that you'll need to see a beautiful history

A beautiful history, a beautiful history

As this song was playing, I was sobbing and praying. Then suddenly I felt the dark cloud lifting up and felt the wonderful embrace and presence of my savior covering my life once again. Jesus soaked my soul into that peace that passes all understanding. There and then, I knew that I had been forgiven. I was in awe of Him. I couldn't believe how much He loved me. He is a God of many second chances; He is not a man, He does not lie, and never changes. I will always be grateful for my Savior Jesus' suffering at the cross. I pray that I will never let Him go again.

In the years following my son Azariah's birth, God has continued to minister to my heart. He kept me in situations where I totally needed to learn to completely put Him first, and depend on Him without anything else. No friend, no family was now needed to rescue me but only Him. I needed to learn that He is enough and He doesn't need my input in order for Him to help me.

After a while, it felt as though God and I were close again. It was a time for him to bless me: to give me the dream job or a wealthy man who will take care of me and my children. Hello! I needed to be rewarded from all the hard work I have been doing here. Once again, my struggle didn't teach me anything about God. This girl just couldn't seem to learn. Without really recognizing the signs, I once again struggled. This brought on new reactions but yet they seemed familiar. I became cold and indifferent toward God without realizing it. I thought He was still punishing me for all the years I had not listened to Him. I was blind to see the precious blessing and miracles around me that God had brought to my life daily. My self-pity blinded me to see the comforting call from a person I didn't expect who was telling me that they were praying for me. My neighbor was being kind enough to take my children to lunch or fixing my car, driving on empty for 50 miles going to church and back, joy that filled my heart even if I literally have nothing in the fridge or in my account.

My ten-year-old son feels happy and he is grateful even though he has been wearing one pair of shoes for months and months. God taught me to be grateful and trust him no matter what. I am still struggling financially like many single moms on one income but spiritually, I am rich. My heart rejoices over every little miracle God does in my life every day. I have learned to trust God even when I don't see anything. When I feel down, He holds my hands and reminds me where He is taking me. I am so glad He is El Roi, the God who sees me. Now instead of numbing myself with TV shows and social media to escape my problems, I face them with God and seek his immeasurable love.

God has truly shown me who He really is and who He wants me to be. He showed me that all my life I praised Him out of my selfish desires because of what He had provided for me instead of what He deserves. God showed me that He owes me nothing at all. However, because his love is unconditional, He gives me gifts even if I don't deserve anything. Everything I have and I am are gifts, not merits. These gifts don't come because I have been good or not, He brings them because He loves me no matter how sinful I am.

He showed me I was nothing and He is in control of every detail of my life. Through all the trials, He never left me hopeless. Sometimes, He worked at the last minute but He showed up and made sure that I knew that it was Him. He taught me to trust Him with all my heart even when I didn't understand. He taught me to be content even when pain surrounds me. He taught me to enjoy his peace even when every storm in my life is raging.

During my life, thus far, I have faced many trials and I am pretty sure will face more but I thank God for all of them because they bring me closer to God. I can now stand and say with confidence in my heart and my Savior Jesus as witness that nothing in this world can separate me from my King. I have that assurance from Jesus. This goes without saying that I will walk to live a blameless life. I won't be perfect until I am with my King but I know that in all the mistakes I will still keep Him first. My constant prayer in my heart is to "… demolish argument and every pretension that sets itself up against the knowledge of God and I take captive every thought to make it obedient to Christ." 2 Corinthians 10:2. "Search me, God and know my heart; test me and know my anxious thoughts. See if there is any offensive way in me and lead me in the way everlasting." Psalm 139:23-24.

I truly believe God is shaping me into a woman and a mother He wants me to be and I pray that He will keep giving me guidance, wisdom and strength to stay in His word. God has taken away my fear of the unknown. I don't need to know or worry for anything because I know He knows!

Most importantly Jesus has taken that place I had once reserved for my sons' father. The good news is that I now no longer live a double life – neither going around hunting for a man, as for now Jesus has my undivided heart. My heart is full and I live a guilt-free life. If God decides to bless us with another man, one who would be my partner and a good parent for my boys; we will welcome him with open arms. If not, I have no fear because I know God will make a way for my family.

God has still not reconciled the relationship I could have had with Hunter. Hunter is still completely estranged with his children by choice. However, I don't worry about it much anymore. Jesus has given me peace about it. Alexander, even at eleven years old, is still too young to fully understand or be affected by his actions. I pray that by the time he completely understands, God will fill his heart with love and comfort and see Him as his complete Father. Sometimes when Alexander brings him into a conversation, I tell him the truth and sometimes we find ourselves praying for Hunter. My children have always been taught to respect, love and pray for their father. I pray God will show my boys that they belong to Jesus. And Jesus used us to be their parents as a service to Him. If Alexander and Azariah get that and it is engraved in their hearts and mind at their young ages, then nothing I can do or anyone else could do will affect them. Because both my sons will know who they belong to – the one who holds their destiny and their breath in His hands, their Maker and Creator. Neither myself or Hunter can truly decide Alexander's or Azariah's future but Almighty God. I have given all the fear, anger and bitterness to God. God loves my sons more than I love them. He will take care of them.

I feel so blessed and sometimes I cannot contain the joy that God has put in my heart. Though it may sound strange to say, still, "I feel that God has been so easy on me instead of having me paying the ultimate price of being rebellious against Him." He instead blessed me with another son Azariah. I named him Azariah because it means "Helped by God". There is no name better suited for him than that. God used him to save me from my own self-destruction. God healed my wounds twice with my boys – those wounds acquired by the genocide horrors. Through Alexander, God taught me that he loves me unconditionally and nothing can separate me from him. Through Azariah, God showed me strength that I never thought I had; and reminded me even when my strength is gone, He is never leaves me. He is my helper who never runs out. Therefore, Jesus healed my wounds and sealed them with my sons.

At times, and maybe even still, the world has thought of me as a failure. My life has been seen as unfortunate – one that could be referred to as a mistake; but God calls me a warrior and lovely.

I see a bright future with my boys. "See, I am doing a new thing! Now, it springs up, do you not perceive it? I am making a way in the wilderness and stream in wasteland." Isaiah: 43:19 "This is what the LORD Almighty says: 'In a little while I will once more shake the heavens and the earth, the sea and the dry land. I will shake all nations, and what is desired by all nations will come, and I will fill this house with glory,' says the LORD Almighty. 'The silver is mine and the gold is mine,' declares the LORD Almighty. The glory of this present house will be greater than the glory of the former house,' says the LORD Almighty. 'And in this place, I will grant peace,' declares the LORD Almighty. (See Haggai 2)

Could anything top these promises from my Father? *"If God is for us, who can be against us?"* Allons-y 'let's go.'

Made in United States
North Haven, CT
24 June 2022